WHAT EVERY CHRISTIAN SHOULD KNOW ABOUT BIBLE PROPHECY

Rick Yohn

HARVEST HOUSE PUBLISHERS

Eugene, Oregon 97402

WHAT EVERY CHRISTIAN SHOULD KNOW ABOUT BIBLE PROPHECY

Copyright © 1982 by Harvest House Publishers
Eugene, Oregon 97402

Library of Congress Catalog Card Number 81-85895
ISBN 0-89081-311-6

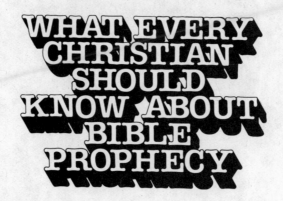

WHAT EVERY CHRISTIAN SHOULD KNOW ABOUT BIBLE PROPHECY

WHAT EVERY CHRISTIAN SHOULD KNOW ABOUT BIBLE PROPHECY

1.

Why Study Prophecy?

Why do most people want to study prophecy? Reasons abound, but probably the greatest driving force is *curiosity*. People have always been curious about the future. Investors consult stock-market analysts to determine where to place their money. Weekend travelers call the weather bureau to determine the advisability for travel. Many people read the daily horoscope and expect their day to follow in accordance with the prediction. Some individuals even involve themselves with self-acclaimed fortune-tellers, prophets, and prophetesses. Curiosity pervades all levels of society. And there is nothing wrong with being curious; even Christ's disciples themselves were motivated in this way.

A. MAN'S MOTIVATION FOR KNOWING THE FUTURE

1. Write the three questions which the disciples asked Jesus outside the temple *(Matthew 24:3)*.

a) _____

_____

_____

b) _____

_____

_____

c) _____

_____

2. Write the question they asked Jesus after His resurrection *(Acts 1:16)*. _____

_____

_____

A second reason why people desire information about the future is that they want to plan effectively in the present. The individual who begins a long trip by car in the winter but is unaware of coming bad weather may find himself stranded in a blizzard. Likewise, many people today are totally unaware of the signs of impending judgment and Jesus' return. They are unprepared spiritually and emotionally to handle what will one day fall upon this planet. Jesus Himself warned of this inability to discern the signs of the times. He rebuked the multitudes by saying, "When you see a cloud rising in the west, immediately you say, 'A shower is coming,' and so it turns out. And when you see a south wind blowing, you say, 'It will be a hot day,' and it turns out that way. You hypocrites! You know how to analyze the appearance of the earth and the sky, but why do you not analyze this present time?'' *(Luke 15:54-56)*.

1. Name three advantages that a person would have by knowing future events.

a) _____

b) _____

c) _____

2. What are some of the disadvantages of not knowing the future?

a) *Matthew 25:1-13* _____

_____

b) *Matthew 24:42-44* _____

_____

c) *Matthew 24:45-51* _____

_____

B. GOD'S MOTIVATION FOR REVEALING THE FUTURE

Curiosity and effective planning for the present are not the only motivating forces which drive people to peer into the future. Other factors could be added, but let's focus on what God expects of people who know the future. Have you ever considered why God reveals future events in the first place? Consider the following factors which should motivate us to focus on the future.

8

1. Fulfilled prophecy informs you who God is.

a) When Daniel interpreted the future for King Nebuchadnezzar, the king replied that God is _____ *(Daniel 2:46,47)*.

b) When King Nebuchadnezzar experienced the fulfillment of God's decree, he learned that

God is sovereign and does according _____

_____ *(Daniel 4:35)*.

c) Nebuchadnezzar responded to God by

_____, _____, and _____ the King of heaven *(Daniel 4:37)*.

d) Nebuchadnezzar also learned that God is

able to _____ *(Daniel 4:37)*.

2. Fulfilled prophecy informs you that unfulfilled predictions will be completed in a literal way as they were in the past.

EVENT	REFERENCE	FULFILLMENT
1. Abram would be the Father of a great nation.	1. *Genesis 12:2* (2000 B.C.)	1. "Now a new king arose over Egypt, who did not know Joseph. And he said to his people, _____ _____ _____ ,, *(Exodus 1:8,9)* (1500 B.C.)
2. Judah would go into captivity.	2. *Isaiah 39:5-8* (710 B.C.)	2. *2 Kings 24:10-16; 25:8-12* (586 B.C.)
3. Judah would return to the land after 70 years of captivity.	3. *Jeremiah 25:11-12* (710 B.C.)	3. "Now in the first year of _____ , in order to fulfill the word of the Lord by the mouth of _____ " *(Ezra 1:1)* "...He has appointed me to _____ in the _____ " *(Ezra 1:2)* (538 B.C.)
4. Jesus would be born in Bethlehem.	4. "But as for you, _____, too little to be among the clans of Judah, from you One will go forth for Me to be ruler in Israel" *(Micah 5:2)* (750 B.C.)	4. "Now after Jesus was born in _____ in the days of Herod the king...." *(Matthew 2:1)* (5-4 B.C.)

3. Fulfilled prophecy verifies the trustworthiness of the Bible.

a) What was the test used to determine whether a man was a true or false prophet *(Deuteronomy 18:20-22)*?

b) Since the Bible has already predicted hundreds of prophecies which have already come true, what do you conclude about the Bible's trustworthiness?

4. Fulfilled prophecy provides comfort for the believer.

a) What did Jesus predict in John 14:1-3?

(1) _____

_____

(2) _____

_____

d) In *1 Thessalonians 4:13-18*, the Apostle Paul informed believers that the Lord had not yet returned. Why did He want them to know that fact *(1 Thessalonians 4:13)*?

_____

b) Which of the two predictions has already been fulfilled?

_____

c) Why did He promise to return for His disciples?

_____

e) For what other reason did Paul inform them that the Lord's return was yet future *(1 Thessalonians 4:18)*? _____

_____

5. Fulfilled prophecy should lead to a more godly and holy life.

It is estimated that Scripture contains 1845 verses concerning Christ's second coming. One out of every 25 verses in the New Testament refers either to the rapture of the church or Christ's second coming to set up His kingdom.

Many of these passages conclude with an exhortation for the believer to lead a more godly lifestyle. Dr. J. Dwight Pentecost writes about his observation of this fact by saying, "A short time ago, I took occasion to go through the New Testament to mark each reference to the coming of the Lord Jesus Christ and to observe the use made of that teaching about His coming. I was struck anew with the fact that almost without exception, when the coming of Christ is mentioned in the New Testament, it is followed by an exhortation to godliness and holy living" *(Prophecy for Today*, p. 19).

In the following passages, first read the prophecy concerning Jesus' return and then write out the exhortation to godly living which either precedes or follows the prophecy.

PREDICTION	EXHORTATION
1. *1 Corinthians 15:50-57*	1. *1 Corinthians 15:58*
2. *1 Thessalonians 2:13*	2. *1 Thessalonians 2:12*
3. *1 Peter 1:13*	3. *1 Peter 1:14-16*
4. *1 Peter 5:4*	4. *1 Peter 5:1-3*
5. *2 Peter 3:10*	5. *2 Peter 3:11,14,17,18*

Why study prophecy? Because of mere curiosity and the personal advantage that you will receive by putting your house in order? These reasons are valid, but God has more important motives for revealing the future to those who are interested enough to investigate the facts.

You should approach this prophetic Bible study with the following objectives in mind:

1. To gain greater insight into the Person of God.

2. To develop the basic assumption that prophecy yet unfulfilled will be completed on schedule, exactly as God has predicted it.

3. To increase your confidence in the Bible's accuracy and trustworthiness.

4. To experience God's comfort, especially during times of testing, realizing that He is working according to a plan.

5. To experience a more godly and holy life in both attitude and behavior.

I want to encourage you, as you approach the rest of this book on prophecy, to make these Biblical objectives your own. Then you will avoid the danger of mere head knowledge by transferring truth into love. Like the Apostle Paul would say, "...knowledge makes arrogant, but love edifies" *(1 Corinthians 8:1)*.

Now prepare yourself for an exciting study of God's look into the future.

Prophecy: Past and Future

It is common to think of prophecy only in terms of the future, and most of this book will do exactly that. But we must recognize that *all* prophecy was future when it was first given. In fact, it is estimated that one-fourth of the Bible was prophetic (spoke about future events) when first written. Many prophecies have already been fulfilled, while other predictions still await fulfillment. *Fulfilled* prophecy includes those predictions which have been completed, such as the many references to the birth, ministry, death, and resurrection of Jesus Christ. Each prediction was fulfilled literally and in exact detail. There was no merely "spiritual" fulfillment of these prophecies (where events occurred in a nonliteral way). *Unfulfilled* prophecy includes those predictions which focus on the future and have not yet been completed.

In this chapter you will look back into the past for a bird's-eye view of what was predicted and fulfilled. Then you will catch a glimpse of God's future plans for man and the universe, in order to understand what will yet be completed in God's schedule.

This chapter will take you on a prophetic tour of the nation Israel, the Gentile world, and the Person of Jesus Christ. Each of these predictions was completed exactly as it was prophesied.

A. FULFILLED PROPHECY CONCERNING ISRAEL

In each of the passages cited, look up the reference where it is fulfilled and *write out only* that phrase, verse, or verses which indicate its fulfillment.

REFERENCE	PROPHECY	REFERENCE	FULFILLMENT
1. *Genesis 12:2*	"And I will make you a great nation."	*Exodus 1:8,9*	1. _____ _____
2. *Genesis 15:13*	"Your descendants will be strangers in a land that is not theirs, where they will be enslaved and oppressed four hundred years."	*Exodus 12:40*	2. _____ _____
3. *Hosea 8:8,9*	"Israel is swallowed up…for they have gone up to Assyria…."	*2 Kings 17:22-26*	3. _____ _____
4. *Isaiah 39:5-7*	"…All that your fathers have laid up in store for this day shall be carried to Babylon…."	*2 Kings 24:10-14*	4. _____ _____
5. *Isaiah 44:28—45:4*	"It is I who says of Cyrus, 'He is My shepherd! And he will perform all My desire.' And he declares of Jerusalem, 'She will be built,' and of the temple, 'Your foundation will be laid.'"	*Ezra 1:1-4*	5. _____ _____

These predictions concerning Israel and Judah are remarkable, for they were fulfilled to the minutest detail. This is why the Prophets Isaiah, Jeremiah, and Hosea, as well as the other Biblical prophets, are so revered among both Jews and Christians alike. They met the requirements of a true prophet. What they prophesied came to pass.

However, though God had chosen the nation of Israel to be His special people, He did not forget the Gentile nations. Through the prophets of Israel, God spoke to the Gentile nations concerning the future. Perhaps the greatest panorama of Gentile history was forecast by the Prophet Daniel as he interpreted the dreams of a king on several occasions.

B. FULFILLED PROPHECY CONCERNING THE GENTILES

In this portion of the chapter, you will not be looking as much to the Scriptures themselves to confirm their fulfillment. Instead, you can discover the accuracy of these prophetic utterances by looking at history.

In the *second chapter* of the *Book of Daniel*, Nebuchadnezzar, King of Babylon, dreamed several dreams. His spirit was extremely troubled, so he called his magicians, conjurers, sorcerers, and Chaldeans into his presence to interpret the dreams. They failed miserably. So Daniel volunteered to interpret the dreams.

In the *seventh chapter* of *Daniel* the prophet himself saw a dream and vision in his mind as he lay on his bed. Then he wrote down the dream. In the eighth chapter Daniel saw another vision, subsequent to the one which appeared to him previously.

Using the following chart, state what Nebuchadnezzar and Daniel saw. Then write the interpretation of those dreams and visions.

REFERENCE	NEBUCHADNEZZAR'S DREAM	DANIEL'S INTERPRETATION
Daniel 2:31-45	1. _____ 2. _____ 3. _____ 4. _____	1. _____ 2. _____ 3. _____ 4. _____

REFERENCE	DANIEL'S DREAM	THE INTERPRETATION
Daniel 7:3-7,10-28	1. _____ 2. _____ 3. _____ 4. _____ 5. _____	1. _____ 2. _____ 3. _____ 4. _____ 5. _____
Daniel 8:3-8,20-22	1. _____ 2. _____	1. _____ 2. _____

As you've noticed, Daniel is describing the four major world powers which would emerge into human history. Each great nation would be supplanted by another one. The fourth nation would become the most dominant and devastating of all (Daniel 7:19).

Later that fourth kingdom would revive into a ten-nation confederacy. But that is future prophecy, which you'll delve into in another chapter. In Daniel chapters two and seven there was a fifth power (Daniel 2:44,45; 7:21,22), which is also future.

But how does history confirm these prophecies? A quick glance into history unveils the fact that Babylon became a world empire in 606 B.C., when it conquered Egypt. The head of that world kingdom was Nebuchadnezzar.

The second kingdom described in the king's vision as silver and in Daniel's vision as a bear (and later as the ram) was the Medo-Persian empire. This world power conquered the Babylonian empire around 530 B.C.

The third great power emerged under the leadership of Alexander the Great, when in 331 B.C. he conquered the Persian empire, bringing Greece to its zenith.

Then in 68 B.C. Rome conquered Greece and the world, becoming the greatest empire to that date.

God is not finished with the Gentile nations. In fact, you are living in a period referred to by Scripture as the "times of the Gentiles" (Luke 21:24). It is the Gentiles to whom Paul became a preacher and an apostle (Galatians 1:16). Today you reap the benefits of God's plan, which grants salvation to all who call upon the Lord (Acts 17:30).

Prophecies concerning Israel and Judah were fulfilled. Prophecies concerning the Gentile powers were likewise fulfilled. Now consider the prophecies concerning the life of the Lord Jesus Christ. They are too numerous to record in this brief chapter, so they will be limited to one each surrounding His birth, ministry, death, burial, resurrection, and ascension, all of which are included in past prophecy.

C. PROPHECIES CONCERNING JESUS CHRIST

In this section follow the same procedure you used under the prophecies about Israel and Judah. Look up the references where the predictions are fulfilled and *write out only* that phrase, verse, or verses which indicate their fulfillment.

REFERENCE	PROPHECY	REFERENCE	FULFILLMENT
1. *Isaiah 7:14*	"Behold, a virgin will be with child and bear a son, and she will call His name Immanuel."	*Matthew 1:18, 23,25*	1. _____
2. *Isaiah 61:1,2*	"The Spirit of the Lord God is upon Me, because the Lord has anointed Me to bring good news to the afflicted."	*Luke 4:16-20*	2. _____
3. *Psalm 22:1,7, 16,18*	"My God, My God, why hast Thou forsaken Me? All who see Me sneer at Me….They wag the head….They pierced My hands and My feet….They divide My garments among them, and for My clothing they cast lots."	*Matthew 27:35, 39,46; John 20:25*	3. _____
4. *Isaiah 53:9*	"His grave was assigned to be with wicked men, yet He was with a rich man in His death."	*Matthew 27: 57-60*	4. _____
5. *Psalm 16:9-11*	"Thou wilt not abandon My soul to Sheol; neither wilt Thou allow Thy Holy One to see the pit."	*Acts 2:22-27*	5. _____
6. *Psalm 68:18*	"Thou hast ascended on high, Thou hast led captive Thy captives."	*Acts 1:9-11; Eph. 4:8-10*	6. _____

You've quickly scanned some of the many prophecies which have already occurred. But many events recorded by the ancient prophets remain unfulfilled. The rest of this chapter will provide a panoramic view of those events.

Perhaps the greatest controversy among Bible scholars and students is not so much concerning *what* is to take place as it is *when* these events will happen. Therefore, consider the major sequence of events portrayed by Jesus, Paul, and John.

1. Jesus' sequence of future events *(Matthew 24, 25)*

a) Birthpangs *(24:4-8)*

b) Tribulation *(24:9-28)*

c) Second coming *(24:29-31)*

d) Judgment *(25:31-46)*

2. Paul's sequence of future events *(2 Thessalonians 2:1-12)*

a) Our gathering together to the Lord *(2:1)*

b) The removal of the Restrainer *(2:6,7)*

c) The apostasy and the Antichrist revealed *(2:3b,4, 8-12)*

d) The coming of the day of the Lord *(2:2b,3a)*

3. John's sequence of future events *(The Book of Revelation)*

a) Present time *(Revelation 1—3)*

b) Saints in heaven *(Revelation 4, 5)*

   (The church is mentioned 39 times in chapters 1—5, but not even once in chapters 6—19.)

c) Tribulation *(Revelation 6—18)*

d) Second coming *(Revelation 19)*

e) Judgment *(Revelation 20)*

f) Eternity *(Revelation 21, 22)*

It is interesting to see the similarities of each sequence. Two of them reveal something about the time in which you are presently living. All three sequences focus on the next worldwide event which will be experienced by unbelievers—the tribulation period, in which the Antichrist rules supreme. Then the Lord returns and brings judgment upon the nations and sets up His kingdom on earth.

This still excludes a lot of other future events which must fit somewhere in the large picture. For example, the Bible refers to several resurrections and several judgments. It talks about a wedding and a great marriage feast. It speaks about Russia invading Israel, and a great battle known as Armageddon.

You'll discover more about these specifics as you continue to read through this book. But before you advance to the next chapter, reflect on the following questions, and write your answers in the available space or on a sheet of paper.

REFLECTIVE QUESTIONS

1. In what way has this chapter given you a greater appreciation for the Bible?

_____

_____

_____

2. What new insight have you gained through this chapter? _____

_____

_____

3. How does it make you feel to know that God has man's history planned?

_____

_____

_____

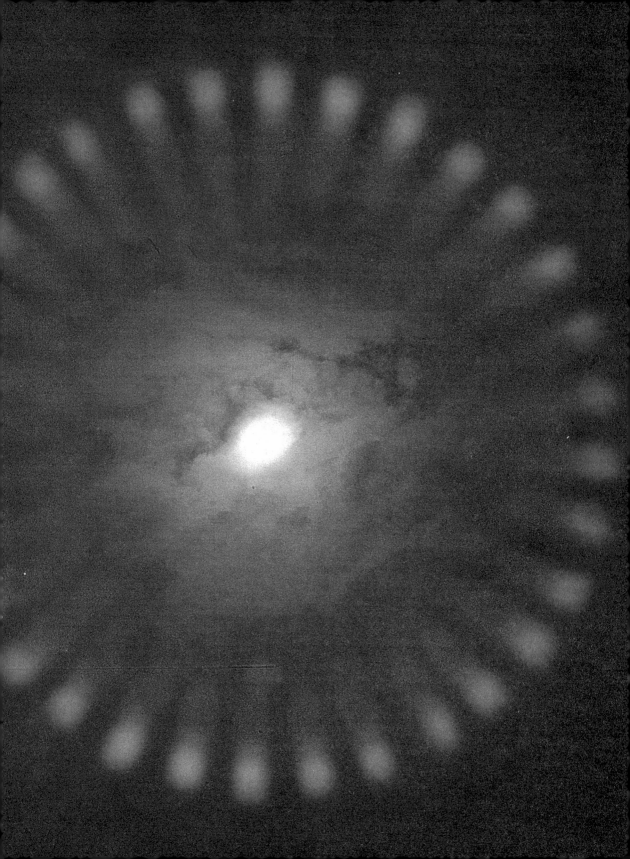

3.

The Great Escape

ack in the 1960's a dramatic film was released entitled *The Great Escape*, which told of Allies in a German prisoner-of-war camp. Half of the film depicted the painstaking plans and effort to dig a tunnel under the barbwire fence and into the nearby woods. The other half of the film related the tragic events after the escape, in which most of the POW's were recaptured. Many of them were shot en masse while others were brought back to the camp.

The Bible describes a future event that will be truly a great escape from Planet Earth. But in this venture no one will be recaptured. Many Bible students refer to this dramatic occurrence as the rapture of the church. This precise term is not found in the Bible, but is a theological term used to describe an unprecedented event of human history. The rapture event occurs in several Scripture passages, but the major passage is *1 Thessalonians 4:13-18*. The phrase "caught up" *(1 Thessalonians 4:17* NASB*)* is the Greek word *arpazo* — "to carry off," "snatch away," "seize for oneself."

This word is used to describe the time when the Holy Spirit snatched Philip from the presence of the Ethiopian eunuch: "And he ordered the chariot to stop; and they both went down into the water, Philip as well as the eunuch; and he baptized him. And when they came up out of the water the Spirit of the Lord *snatched* Philip away; and the eunuch saw him no more, but went on his way rejoicing" *(Acts 8:38,39)*. At one moment Philip was speaking with the Ethiopian, but at the next he had vanished.

That's how it's going to be at the rapture. Two people will be driving in a car, a believer and unbeliever. When the rapture occurs, the believer will vanish. The unbeliever will remain behind, but he won't be rejoicing. If he's driving the car, he'll have difficulty controlling his fear as he attempts to pull to the side of the road. If the Christian was driving, the unbeliever will be in even worse condition as the car goes careening off the road.

A. OLD TESTAMENT ILLUSTRATIONS OF THE RAPTURE

Even though the rapture of the church is not mentioned in the Old Testament, two events provide interesting similarities between what happened to two men of God and what will happen to believers at the time of the rapture.

1. Read *Genesis 5:24*.

2. Who walked with God? _____

3. What happened to this man of God? Why?

_____

_____

4. Read *Hebrews 11:5*.

5. What did he not experience? _____

_____

6. How long do you think that event took? _____

_____

7. What was not left behind? _____

_____

8. Read *2 Kings 2:11*.

9. Who vanished this time? _____

_____

10. Where did he go? _____

_____

11. How did he get there? _____

_____

_____

12. What was left behind *(2 Kings 2:12,13)*?

_____

_____

13. What couldn't the sons of the prophets find *(2 Kings 2:15-18)*?

_____

_____

B. NEW TESTAMENT PROPHECIES CONCERNING THE RAPTURE

Now notice how closely those Old Testament illustrations resemble the New Testament predictions. This section will be limited to three basic passages which speak of that great escape, though several others could be cited.

1. Read *John 14:1-4*.

Jesus is preparing His disciples for the tragic events which are about to unfold before their eyes. Within the evening, this One who claimed to be Messiah and was believed by the disciples to be the very Son of God would be taken away for a mock trial and crucifixion.

The Lord informed His bewildered followers that He was going to prepare a place for them. And then He made a special promise: ''And if I go and prepare a place for you, I will come again, and receive you to Myself; that where I am, there you may be also'' *(John 14:3)*. Focus on the threefold promise: a) Jesus would return; b) He would receive them to Himself; c) wherever He is, they would be with Him.

2. Read *1 Thessalonians 4:13-18*.

3. What will the Lord do *(1 Thessalonians 4:16)*?

_____

_____

4. What will the dead believers do?

(1 Thessalonians 4:16)? _____

_____

5. What will living believers do *(1 Thessalonians 4:17)*? _____

_____

6. Where will both groups of believers meet the Lord *(1 Thessalonians 4:17)*?

a) _____

_____

b) _____

_____

7. How long will the believers remain with Jesus *(1 Thessalonians 4:17)*? _____

_____

8. Read *1 Corinthians 15:50-58*.

In this passage the Apostle Paul informs his readers that flesh and blood cannot enter heaven. Something has to change before you can make it through those golden gates, even though you are a born-again Christian.

9. What is going to change *(1 Corinthians 15:51,53)*? _____

_____

_____

_____

10. How long will that change take *(1 Corinthians 15:52)*? _____

_____

_____

_____

11. Name the three phases which will take place simultaneously *(1 Corinthians 15:52)*.

a) _____

_____

b) _____

_____

c) _____

_____

The phrase translated ''in a moment'' comes from the Greek word *atom*, from which we get the word ''atom.''

Have you noticed the similarities between the Old Testament illustrations and the New Testament prophecies concerning the rapture?

12. List at least five similarities between the illustrations and prophecies, as well as between the three New Testament passages themselves.

a) _____

b) _____

c) _____

d) _____

e) _____

Though you may be wondering at this point *when* the rapture will occur, I want to save the time sequence for a later chapter. But at this point it's important to notice that two terms are often used interchangeably, and yet they speak of different events. Those terms are: a) the rapture, and b) the second coming.

Sometimes the phrase "second coming" is used to describe two parts of Christ's return—first, to snatch away the saints, and second, to return to earth and set up His kingdom. But it is better not to blend the terms into one idea.

C. THE RAPTURE AND THE SECOND COMING: TWO DISTINCT EVENTS

By using the following chart and reading each reference, write out the distinctions which you discover between the two separate events.

THE RAPTURE	THE SECOND COMING
1. The purpose of the rapture is "to snatch away." He is coming to remove believers from earth.	1. The purpose of the second coming is described in *2 Thessalonians 1:7,8* as a time for _____.
2. Jesus comes in the air for the saints *(1 Thessalonians 4:17)*.	2. Jesus comes to _____ and His feet stand on _____ _____ *(Zechariah 14:4)*.
3. The church is taken out of the earth to be with Jesus in heaven *(1 Thessalonians 4:17)*.	3. Jesus comes and establishes His _____ _____ upon the earth *(Acts 15:16-18)*.
4. The rapture is a message of comfort *(1 Thessalonians 4:18)*.	4. The second coming is a message of _____ _____ _____ *(Revelation 6:12-17)*.
5. The rapture is a mystery (never revealed in the Old Testament) *(1 Corinthians 15:51)*.	5. The second coming is not a mystery, because it was foretold many times in the Old Testament.

D. PREPARATION FOR THE RAPTURE

You've learned that the rapture is the event describing Jesus' return in the air to snatch away *the church*, the body of Christ, from the earth. Therefore, not every person on earth will be taken.

1. Read *1 Thessalonians 4:14*.

2. What is the requirement to become part of the rapture? _____

_____

_____

_____

_____

3. How is this requirement described in *John 1:12*? _____

_____

_____

_____

_____

4. *Romans 10:9,10* describes it another way: "That if you _____ with your mouth _____ _____, and _____ in your heart that God raised Him from the dead, you shall be _____ _____; for with the heart man believes, resulting in _____; and with the mouth, he confesses, resulting in _____."

5. According to these verses, who are the only people who will take part in the rapture?

_____

_____

_____

_____

_____

_____

_____

6. Will you be taken or left behind? _____

7. How do you know? _____

_____

_____

_____

_____

_____

I trust that you are going to be part of the great escape. If you have any doubts, you can make sure that you will be part of it by praying this prayer with a sincere heart:

Dear Lord, I do believe that Jesus is God and that He died for my sins. I don't deserve Your love and salvation. I confess that I have sinned against You, and I turn away from my sin to serve You and live for You. Please come into my life and forgive all my sins. Make me the person You want me to be. Thank You, Jesus, for coming into my life right now. I believe that You have answered my prayer. In Jesus' name I pray, Amen.

If you have sincerely invited Jesus Christ into your life, I congratulate you and say, "Welcome to the family of God." When we go up, you'll go up to be with us to meet the Lord in the air. And we'll forever be with the Lord.

The Great Holocaust

In the midst of intense emotion, survivors of the great Nazi holocaust met in Jerusalem on June 14, 1981, for the first holocaust reunion. With numbers tattooed on their arms and tragic memories eternally etched in their minds, the 6000 survivors laughed, cried, embraced, and gave thanks for escaping the victims' list of six million people who perished in Auschwitz, Brichenwald, Dachau, and other concentration camps.

Many people consider those years of Jewish genocide, as the most severe testing which any people will ever have to endure. In the same month of the holocaust reunion, Israel destroyed Iraq's nuclear reactor, claiming that Iraq planned to make atomic bombs and destroy Israel. During a press conference, Prime Minister Menachem Begin justified the raid by saying, "There will never be another holocaust. Never."

The Jewish nation has indeed experienced great tragedy. Every day that an Israeli awakens, he recognizes that it may be his last. The entire Mideast region is a powder keg waiting for someone to light the fuse. And as much as Israel wants to avoid a repeat of the tragedies experienced in those Nazi concentration camps, another holocaust is inevitable. Only this time it won't come from Nazi Germany, but from the tyrannical Bear in the north. And great destruction will not be limited to Israel alone. The entire world will feel an unprecedented outpouring of death and devastation.

A. HOW IS THIS GREAT HOLOCAUST DESCRIBED IN SCRIPTURE?

1. Read *Matthew 24:15-28*.

2. How does Jesus describe this period of world-wide destruction (*Matthew 24:21,22*)?

_____

_____

_____

_____

3. Look up the following passages and write the description of the dreadful future period of man's history.

a) *Zephaniah 1:18* — Day of _____

b) *Isaiah 24:1-4* — The earth will be completely

_____

and completely _____

_____

c) *Daniel 12:1* — A time of _____

_____

d) *Joel 2:1-3* — A day of _____

_____

e) *Revelation 3:10* — The hour of _____

_____

As you can see from these descriptions, the world hasn't seen anything yet to compare with what it will eventually experience. The world will finally taste God's wrath, which justifiably will be poured out on man because of his utter rejection of God.

B. HOW LONG WILL THE HOLOCAUST LAST?

One of the evidences for the unity of Scripture is that different writers spanning many centuries describe the same future event with uncanny similarity. For example, Daniel and John the Apostle were both Jewish prophets. However, Daniel lived 700 years before John. Yet, as both describe the time span of future tribulation, they come to the same conclusion.

Look up the following references, and write out the description of time.

1. *Daniel 7:25* _____

_____

_____

_____

2. *Daniel 9:24,25,27* _____

3. *Daniel 12:7* _____

_____

_____

_____

4. *Revelation 11:2; 13:5* _____

_____

_____

_____

5. *Revelation 11:3* _____

_____

_____

_____

6. *Revelation 12:6* _____

_____

_____

_____

7. *Revelation 12:14* _____

_____

_____

_____

"A time, times, and half a time" seems very mysterious, and yet it's really very simple. "A time" is one, "times" are two, and "half a time" is one-half. So all that we know from the first description by Daniel and the last description by John is that they are referring to 3½ something. It could be hours, days, weeks, months, or years.

But Daniel writes, "*Seventy weeks* have been decreed for your people and your holy city, to finish the transgression, to make an end of sin, to make atonement for iniquity, to bring in everlasting righ-

teousness, to seal up vision and prophecy, and to anoint the most holy place. So you are to know and discern that from the issuing of a decree to restore and rebuild Jerusalem [Cyrus in 445 B.C.] until Messiah the Prince [4-5 A.D.], there will be *seven weeks* and *sixty-two weeks* [69 weeks of years]; it will be built again, with plaza and moat, even in times of distress. Then after the *sixty-two weeks*, the Messiah will be cut off and have nothing [Jesus crucified about 26-28 A.D.], and the people of the prince who is to come [Antiochus — 70 A.D.] will destroy the city and the sanctuary. And its end will come with a flood; even to the end there will be war; desolations are determined. And he will make a firm covenant with the many for *one week* [seven years], but in the *middle of the week* [3½ years], he will put a stop to sacrifice and grain offering; and on the wing of abominations will come one who makes desolate [Antichrist], even until a complete destruction, one that is decreed, is poured out on the one who makes desolate" *(Daniel 9:24-27)*.

Between *Daniel 9:26* and *9:27* there is a gap of time. We know this to be true because historically the Messiah was cut off (27 A.D.) and the city of Jerusalem with its temple was destroyed (70 A.D.). However, no ruler has yet made a firm covenant with Israel for one week (seven years). Nor has the temple been rebuilt. Nor have sacrifices begun in

Israel. These events are yet future and will last for one week of a seven-year duration. The last week (seventieth week) of this prophecy has yet to be fulfilled. The time from Jesus' crucifixion up to today is not mentioned in this prophecy.

But a day is predicted when a world ruler will repeat the atrocities of Antiochus, who devastated the holy city and its people in 70 A.D. There will indeed be another holocaust which falls upon God's chosen nation.

To further prove that the duration of the tribulation is a seven-year period, with the greater atrocities on Israel and worldwide devastation in the last 3½ years, all we need to do is divide 42 months by 12, or 1260 days by 360 (days in a prophetic year), and we will conclude with 3½ years.

C. WHAT EVENTS WILL OCCUR DURING THIS PERIOD OF SEVEN YEARS?

1. The rise of four major national powers

a) Read *Daniel 11:36-45*.

b) The king of *11:36* is the king of the West (Antichrist).

c) What other three kings are mentioned?

(1)_____

_____

(2)_____

_____

(3)_____

_____

These kings will be described in a later chapter, when we focus on the subject of Armageddon.

2. Preaching throughout the world

The tribulation period is a time of great evangelistic effort throughout the world. Jesus said, "And this gospel of the kingdom shall be preached in the whole world for a witness to all the nations, and then the end shall come" *(Matthew 24:14)*. Some commentators believe that this statement refers to the present age. I believe that this is a possibility, but I prefer to interpret "the end" as referring to the end of the period preceding Jesus' return to earth *(Matthew 24:3,6,14)*. That period is the seven-year tribulation. At the same time, it is evident that what we are seeing today in the expanse of the "electronic church," with the gospel beaming all over the world by satellite, is probably the beginning of this prophecy's fulfillment.

a) According to *Revelation 11:3*, how long do God's two witnesses evangelize?

_____

_____

b) According to *Revelation 14:1-3*, how many other evangelists does God send forth to preach?

_____

_____

c) Describe the 144,000 evangelists *(Revelation 7:4-10; 14:1-5)*. _____

_____

_____

_____

Besides the rise of four major military powers and worldwide evangelism, the tribulation will also include the establishing and breaking of a peace treaty.

3. The establishing and breaking of a peace treaty

About the only friend that Israel has left today is the United States. At the beginning of the tribulation period, the leader of the Western power will make a peace treaty with Israel *(Daniel 9:27)*. At that point Israel will feel safe. They will finally begin to relax, with a sense of political and military security.

But in the midst of that false security the Western leader will break his treaty and set himself up as an object of worship. He will be a man of tremendous charisma. The whole world will be overwhelmed by his great powers and abilities, and they will actually worship him as a god: "The whole earth was amazed and followed after the beast; and they worshiped the dragon [Satan], because he gave his authority to the beast; and they worshiped the beast, saying, 'Who is like the beast, and who is able to wage war with him?'" *(Revelation 13:3,4)*.

a) From whom does this beast receive his power *(Revelation 13:2)*? _____

_____

b) How does this beast treat those who come to Christ during the tribulation *(Revelation 13:7; 7:13,14)*? _____

_____

_____

_____

_____

c) How long is this ruler in absolute power *(Revelation 13:5)*? _____

_____

_____

_____

This same chapter indicates that there will be a second beast who works alongside the first. He is a religious leader who has the ability to perform miracles, and he causes men to worship the first beast (the political ruler).

d) What else does he demand *(Revelation 13:16,17)*? _____

_____

_____

_____

_____

e) What is the number of the beast?

_____

f) If a person refuses the number, what is his fate *(Revelation 13:17)*? _____

_____

_____

_____

_____

There are three other major events which occur during this dreadful outpouring of God's wrath upon the earth. One of them is the wrath of God poured out on the earth in the form of seven seal judgments, seven trumpet judgments, and seven vial judgments. These judgments will be discussed in the next chapter.

Another great event at the end of the great tribulation is that awesome last battle of mankind which even the world now acknowledges as inevitable, the Battle of Armageddon. This event also will be highlighted in another chapter.

Now let's concentrate on one more major event during that tribulation period—the ten-nation confederacy.

4. The ten-nation confederacy

In a previous chapter you read about the dream of the Babylonian king, Nebuchadnezzar. As Daniel interpreted the dream, he informed the king that he had seen a multimetalled image in his dream comprised of gold, silver, bronze, and iron, which had feet mixed with iron and clay. Each metal represented a kingdom, and history has confirmed that four successive kingdoms became world powers: Babylonia, Medo-Persia, Greece, and Rome.

The final form of the fourth kingdom was ten toes of iron and clay *(Daniel 2:41)*. In Daniel's vision the final form of the fourth kingdom was a beast with ten horns. In *Daniel 7:23-25* the prophet interprets the vision: ''Thus he said: 'The fourth beast will be a fourth kingdom on the earth, which will be different from all the other kingdoms, and it will devour the whole earth and tread it down and crush it. As for the ten horns, out of the kingdom ten kings will arise; and another will arise after them, and he will be different from the previous ones and will subdue three kings. And he will speak out against the Most High and wear down the saints of the Highest One, and he will intend to make alterations in times and in law; and they will be given into his hand for a time [one], times [two], and half a time [one-half].''

a) Read *Revelation 17:3*.

b) How many horns are on the scarlet beast?

_____

c) Who are the ten horns and what do they do, according to *Revelation 17:12*?

_____

_____

_____

_____

_____

_____

_____

_____

_____

d) How many horns are on the dragon of *Revelation 12:3*? _____

e) Who then gives these ten kings their authority?

_____

Who are these ten kings? They are the leaders of the ten nations which were originally in the old Roman Empire. What sign do we have today of such a ten-nation confederacy? We don't have to look very far. In January 1981, Greece became the tenth nation to enter the European Common Market, which is made up entirely of nations which were at one time part of the old Roman Empire!

5. Worldwide Fireworks

Who will ever forget that beautiful display of fireworks over the Washington monument on July 4, 1976? What exquisite color! What deafening, explosive sound! It was the once-in-a-lifetime celebration of America's Bicentennial. As the rockets were launched into the air, you could see first one explosion which looked like a colorful umbrella, and then, as it began to die out, another explosion which cracked with a second brilliant umbrella. As soon as it faded, a third explosion produced still another dazzling umbrella.

The tribulation judgment will be poured forth like that. First a series of seven seal judgments will come. Then out of the seventh seal a series of seven trumpet judgments will explode onto the earth. And out of the seventh trumpet judgment will come seven vial judgments.

These judgments are revealed in *Revelation chapters 6, 8, 9,* and *16.* Consider these judgments of God in three phases.

A. PHASE ONE: THE SEVEN SEAL JUDGMENTS *(Revelation 6)*

In the *fifth chapter* of *Revelation*, the Apostle John saw a seven-sealed book, but no one could be found worthy enough to open it. Then John saw a Lamb standing, and He came and took the book as though He had the authority to open it. John continues, "And when He had taken the book, the four living creatures and the twenty-four elders fell down before the Lamb, having each one a harp, and golden bowls full of incense, which are the prayers of the saints. And they sang a new song, saying, "Worthy art Thou to take the book, and to break its seals; for Thou wast slain, and didst purchase for God with Thy blood men from every tribe and tongue and people and nation" *(Revelation 5:8,9).*

In the *sixth chapter* of *Revelation* the Lamb breaks the first seal.

As you continue to read *Revelation 6,* fill out the information requested on the following chart.

REFERENCE	COLOR OF HORSE	RIDER'S TOOLS	RIDER'S NAME	RIDER'S PURPOSE
1. *Revelation 6:1,2* Seal 1				
2. *Revelation 6:3,4* Seal 2				
3. *Revelation 6:5,6* Seal 3				
4. *Revelation 6:7,8* Seal 4				

These four riders are often referred to as the four horsemen of the Apocalypse. They bring tremendous devastation upon the earth.

1. How does the fifth seal differ from the others?

_____

_____

_____

2. How extensive was the earthquake in the sixth seal? _____

_____

_____

3. How does unbelieving man respond to God's wrath? _____

_____

_____

The chapter ends with the sixth seal judgment. *Chapter 7* of *Revelation* is like a parenthesis and does not follow chronologically after *chapter 6*. But when you turn to *Revelation chapters 8* and *9*, you'll pick up where you left off in *chapter 6*.

B. PHASE TWO: THE SEVEN TRUMPET JUDGMENTS *(Revelation 8,9)*

Notice that when the seventh seal is broken, nothing seems to happen. It's like the fireworks which begin to fade, and then POW!

Trace through *chapters 8* and *9*, and write down which "one-third" is being destroyed.

1. First trumpet *(Revelation 8:7)*

A third of the earth, a third of the trees, and all green grass was burned up.

2. Second trumpet *(Revelation 8:8,9)*

_____

_____

3. Third trumpet *(Revelation 8:10,11)*

_____

_____

4. Fourth trumpet *(Revelation 8:12,13)*

_____

_____

As in Phase One four horsemen were followed by two other kinds of judgments, so Phase Two introduces four trumpet judgments which bring a devastating effect on one-third of creation. These judgments are followed by two other trumpets, which produce a different type of judgment.

5. Fifth trumpet *(Revelation 9:1-12)*

a) Describe the creatures which issue out of this

trumpet. _____

_____

_____

_____

_____

_____

b) What is their purpose? _____

_____

_____

6. Sixth trumpet *(Revelation 9:13-21)*

a) How much of mankind is killed? _____

_____

b) How did the rest of mankind respond to these

judgments? _____

_____

_____

_____

Again, the seventh trumpet judgment is not given in *Revelation 9*. However, the next few chapters give a preview of things to come: "In the days of the voice of the *seventh angel*, when he is about to sound, then the mystery of God is finished, as He preached to His servants the prophets....And the *seventh angel* sounded....And I saw another sign in heaven, great and marvelous, *seven angels* who had seven plagues, which are the last, because in them the wrath of God is finished'' *(Revelation 10:7; 11:15; 15:1)*. Now in *Revelation 16* the final phase is about to begin.

C. PHASE THREE: THE SEVEN BOWL JUDGMENTS *(Revelation 16)*

In these final judgments, write a brief description (one to five words) of each vial.

1. First bowl *(Revelation 16:2)*

_____

_____

_____

2. Second bowl *(Revelation 16:3)*

_____

_____

3. Third bowl *(Revelation 16:4-7)*

_____

_____

_____

4. Fourth bowl *(Revelation 16:8,9)*

_____

_____

_____

5. Fifth bowl *(Revelation 16:10,11)*

_____

_____

_____

6. Sixth bowl *(Revelation 16:12-15)*

_____

_____

_____

7. Seventh bowl *(Revelation 16:17-21)*

_____

_____

_____

8. How did men respond to these judgments?

_____

_____

_____

_____

The greatest tragedy resulting from these judgments is not the devastation which man and nature experiences, though that is terrible in itself. An even greater tragedy is the way men respond to God's righteous and justifiable wrath.

In the first series of judgments, they run and attempt to hide from God, as Adam and Eve did in the Garden after they had sinned. After the second series of judgments, men refuse to repent of their murders, sorceries, immoralities, and thefts. They continue in their sin. Following the final series of judgments, men blaspheme God. They are irreversibly hardened. They hate God and will not come to Him for mercy and salvation. They only shake their fists in His face and call Him names.

If you have not yet come to know God in a personal way, do not postpone your decision. ''Today if you hear His voice, do not harden your hearts, as when they [Israel] provoked Me'' *(Hebrews 3:15)*. Jesus says, ''Behold, I stand at the door and knock; if any one hears My voice and opens the door, I will come in to him, and will dine with him, and he with Me'' *(Revelation 3:20)*.

If there is any doubt in your mind whether Jesus lives in your life, why not pray the following prayer with a sincere heart:

Dear Jesus, I invite You to come into my life. I believe that You are God. I confess that I have sinned against You, and I ask for Your forgiveness. I turn from my sin and ask that You help me to live for You. Please make me what I can be and what You want me to be. I pray in Jesus' name. Amen.

If you have invited Jesus into your life for the first time (you only need to do it once), why not tell someone, or write to me: Rick Yohn, P. O. Box 9550, Fresno, California 93793. I will gladly send you some follow-up material that will help you in your new Christian life.

6. The Coming World Dictator

What do the names Napoleon, Hitler, and Stalin have in common with the names Kennedy, Kissinger, and Sadat? Each of these individuals has been declared a prime candidate as the Antichrist by some well-meaning but presumptuous Bible students. And to that list several dozen other names have also been suggested.

Today a new surge of interest in a world leader has emerged. People all over the globe are looking for a world hero who will deliver them from the perils of economic strangulation, political chaos, social upheaval, and military paranoia.

The craving for a world superstar can be further seen as a renewed interest in the heroes of yesterday proliferate on TV and the movie screen. A few years ago TV offered *The Six Million Dollar Man, Batman, The Bionic Woman,* and *Wonder Woman*. The film industry captures your imagination through creative special effects as you cheer Luke Skywalker in his battle against Darth Vader and the forces of evil. Or you can fly with Superman or ride with the Lone Ranger and Tonto, and deal a deadly blow to the problems of life.

But that's Fantasyland. What about the real world in which you live? Are people really looking for such a superstar?

A recent report indicates that nearly 25 million North Americans have been swept into the cults in the last decade. In November 1978, 913 ardent followers of a self-appointed messiah (Jim Jones) took their lives in a mass suicide pact. The list of false messiahs continues to grow. Twenty million people believe that Korean Sun Myung Moon is the real Messiah. Other millions are devoted to Hare Krishna, Transcendental Meditation, Scientology, and many other such religious groups, looking for someone to offer the solutions to life's problems.

And that is basically what the coming world dictator will offer the world. Prepare, therefore, to paint your own portrait of this man who will emerge on the world scene in the latter days.

A. THE WORLD DICTATOR'S DESCRIPTION

NAMES

Use the following references and write a one-to-five-word description of the Antichrist.

1. The _____

_____

who is to come *(Daniel 9:26)*.

2. Then the _____

_____

will do as he pleases *(Daniel 11:36)*.

3. Then that _____

_____

will be revealed *(2 Thessalonians 2:8)*.

4. _____
is coming *(1 John 2:18)*.

5. The _____
that comes up out of the abyss *(Revelation 11:7)*.

This coming world dictator is also described in other terms. Read *Revelation 13:1-3*, and list those characteristics attributed to this man.

SYMBOLS

1. _____ horns

2. _____ heads

3. _____ diadems

4. Like a _____

5. Feet like those of a _____

_____

6. Mouth like the mouth of a _____

_____

7. The _____
gave him his power and his throne and great authority.

The horns are symbolic of political power. Therefore, the ten horns picture the ten nations which form a confederacy ruled by the world dictator *(Revelation 17:12)*. The seven heads are seven mountains and seven kings *(Revelation 17:9,10)*. The diadems are the crowns or symbols of authority of the ten kings.

The image of a leopard, bear, and lion are the exact images which Daniel used to describe the first three world empires: Babylon (like a lion) *(Daniel 7:4)*, Medo-Persia (like a bear) *(Daniel 7:5)*, and Greece (like a leopard) *(Daniel 7:6)*. This Antichrist will combine all the characteristics of the previous empires. He will have the regal splendor of a lion, the power of a bear, and the destructive swiftness of a leopard.

This beast which came up out of the sea receives his power from the dragon: "They worshiped the dragon, because he gave his authority to the beast; and they worshiped the beast, saying, 'Who is like the beast, and who is able to wage war with him?'" *(Revelation 13:4)*.

Who is this dragon? According to *Revelation 12:7*, Michael and his angels waged war with the dragon and his angels. At this point you might have guessed at the dragon's identity, but if you read a little further, you'll no longer have to guess at his identity. Write out *Revelation 12:9* in the space below and positively identify the dragon.

The old serpent who tempted Eve at the beginning of man's creation is still working with great fury at the end of man's history, before Jesus returns to Planet Earth.

The coming world dictator will be empowered by Satan to accomplish what no other man has been able to achieve. And much of what he does is an imitation of what Jesus did.

B. THE WORLD DICTATOR'S ACTIVITIES

In the chart below, compare and contrast Jesus Christ and the Antichrist. First read the reference, and then in a few words describe their activities.

JESUS CHRIST	THE ANTICHRIST
1. *Matthew 19:28* _____ _____ _____ _____	1. *Revelation 13:2* _____ _____ _____ _____
2. *1 Corinthians 15:4* _____ _____ _____ _____	2. *Revelation 13:3* _____ _____ _____ _____
3. *Revelation 4:9-11* _____ _____ _____ _____	3. *Revelation 13:4* _____ _____ _____ _____
4. *Philippians 2:9-11* _____ _____ _____	4. *Revelation 13:7* _____ _____ _____

5. *John 14:27* _____

_____

_____

_____

5. *Daniel 9:27* _____

_____

_____

_____

6. *John 10:30-33* _____

_____

_____

_____

6. *2 Thessalonians 2:4* _____

_____

_____

_____

7. *Mark 6:2* _____

_____

_____

_____

7. *2 Thessalonians 2:9* _____

_____

_____

_____

The Antichrist is a false messiah. A counterfeit attempts to look like the real thing. So this future leader will probably appear as a peace-loving individual at the beginning of his political career. He will talk about peace, work for peace, and actually bring about a temporary peace in the Middle East. But in the middle of the seven-year tribulation the scene will change drastically. Paul describes it vividly: "While they are saying, 'Peace and safety!' then destruction will come upon them suddenly, like birth pangs upon a woman with child; and they shall not escape" *(1 Thessalonians 5:3).*

C. THE WORLD DICTATOR'S PARTNER

The Bible reveals that the coming world dictator not only is empowered by Satan but also has an accomplice in his ruling power. Whereas the first beast comes up out of the sea (the Gentile nations), the second beast comes from the earth ("land" is symbolic of the land of Israel or the Middle East).

1. Instead of ten horns, he has

_____ *(Revelation 13:11).*

2. Instead of resembling a leopard, bear, and lion, he looks more like a _____

_____ *(Revelation 13:11).*

3. Who else in Scripture is symbolized by this animal? _____

4. What is his major role *(Revelation 13:12,15)?* _____

_____

_____

_____

5. What other task is he responsible to perform *(Revelation 13:16-18)?* _____

_____

_____

_____

6. What happens to those who receive the mark of the beast *(Revelation 14:9-12)?*

_____

_____

_____

7. What happens to those who refuse to receive the mark *(Revelation 20:4)?* _____

_____

_____

_____

There is a lot of speculation about the mark of the beast. The Bible tells us that the number of the beast is that of a man, and that his number is 666 *(Revelation 13:18)*.

The number 666 is appearing with great frequency throughout the world today. For example, the World Bank code number is 666. New credit cards in the U.S. are now being assigned the prefix 666. The IRS Alcohol, Tobacco and Firearms Division has on their employee badges the number 666. IRS instructions for Non-Profit Corporation Employee 1979, W-2 Forms, requires the prefix 666. The United States Selective Service Cards have 666 on them. Arab-owned vehicles in Jerusalem have license plates prefixed with 666. A record album released by a rock group, Black Sabbath, is named *666.*

What does all this mean? It means that man is getting very comfortable with the 666 number.

In the near future, cash will be obsolete. Ask any economist. Read the latest literature as to how man plans to solve the economic problems of the world. One magazine article after another predicts that every economic transaction will be computerized. Then every person will be given a number which could be invisibly tattooed on his hand or forehead. And with a laser scanner of some type, the number will be identified and the person will be able to buy or sell.

Such laser scanners are not something for the year 2000. They exist today in many of your local supermarkets. The idea of a cashless and eventually cardless society is as fresh as today's magazine articles on finances in the 1980's.

So all systems are go. We are, I believe, in the final countdown. It's just a matter of time before this world experiences a cashless, cardless society.

But what happens after this beast and his false prophet rule over the earth for the last 3½ years of great tribulation?

D. THE WORLD DICTATOR'S FINAL DESTINY

Like the dictators of the past who enjoyed power and fame for a period of time, these men will also come to their end. Jesus Christ will return at the end of the tribulation *(Matthew 24:29,30; Revelation 19:11,19).*

1. What does Christ do with the beast and false prophet *(Revelation 19:20)*? _____

_____

_____

_____

2. What does Christ do with Satan 1000 years later *(Revelation 20:7-10)*? _____

_____

_____

_____

3. What does Christ do with those whose names are not found written in the Book of life *(Revelation 20:11-15)*? _____

_____

_____

_____

_____

The days of the world dictator's rule will be dreadful. But the millions of years after the beast is removed from power will be worse yet for those who have never received Jesus Christ as their personal Savior. It will be an eternity away from God and an eternity with Satan, the beast, the false prophet, and all other unbelievers.

If you have put off making that all-important decision to receive Jesus Christ into your life, I urge you to do so now, in the quietness of your heart. The Bible warns, "Now is the acceptable time; behold, now is the day of salvation" *(2 Corinthians 6:2)*. "Do not boast about tomorrow, for you do not know what a day may bring forth" *(Proverbs 27:1)*.

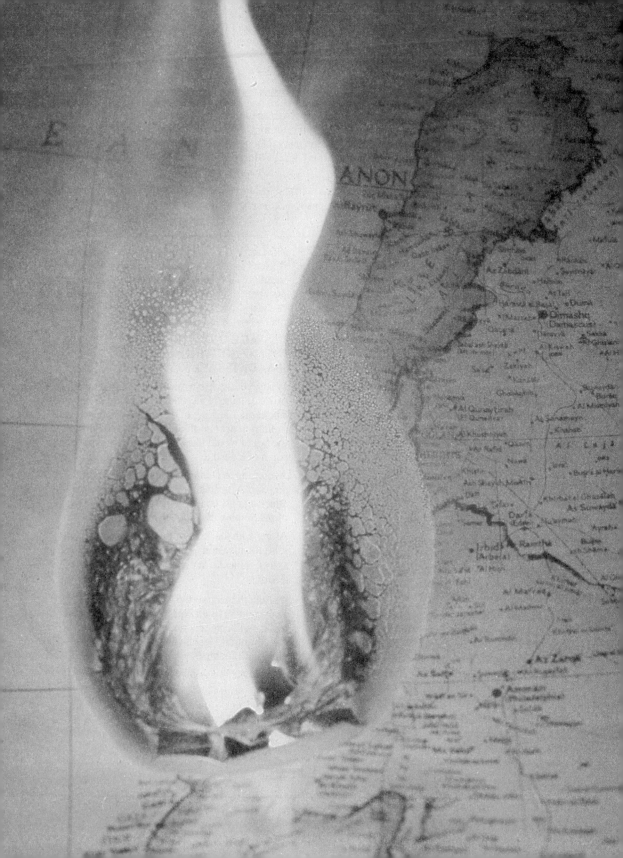

Few words evoke fear in one's heart like the word "Armageddon." Religious and secular authors have written about it. TV news commentators often refer to it. Many politicians and military personnel have resigned themselves to its inevitability. General Douglas MacArthur once warned, "We have had our last chance. The Battle of Armageddon comes next!" Most governments of the world are expecting World War Three. It's just a matter of time.

But what is this Armageddon? When will it take place? Who will be involved in its terrible devastation? This chapter will help you answer these and related questions concerning that last great stupidity of mankind against himself—Armageddon.

A. WHAT DOES ARMAGEDDON MEAN?

The word "Armageddon" comes from a Hebrew word meaning "The Mound of Megiddo," a small mountain 15 miles inland from the Mediterranean Sea and 10 miles south of Nazareth. It overlooks a broad valley 14 miles wide and 20 miles long. This great Plain of Megiddo is referred to as Armageddon and the Valley of Jehoshaphat.

The Apostle John describes this final battle in the Apocalypse *(The Book of Revelation)*: "And the sixth angel poured out his bowl upon the great river, the Euphrates; and its water was dried up, that the way might be prepared for the kings from the east. And I saw coming out of the mouth of the dragon and out of the mouth of the beast, and out of the mouth of the false prophet, three unclean spirits like frogs; for they are spirits of demons, performing signs, which go out to the kings of the whole world, to gather them together for the war of the great day of God, the Almighty. (Behold, I am coming like a thief. Blessed is the one who stays awake and keeps his garments, lest he walk about naked and men see his shame.) *And they gathered them together to the place which in Hebrew is called Har-Magedon*" *(Revelation 16:12-16)*.

From John's description several facts are evident: a) the final battle will be at the end of the great tribulation (the sixth bowl judgment); b) it will occur in and around the Plain of Megiddo, which Napoleon allegedly described as the ideal battleground; c) it is a battle of the world's military powers (the kings of the whole world); d) it is demonically inspired.

What we don't find in this portion of Scripture is that the Armageddon event is the climactic conflict of a series of battles throughout the latter half of the tribulation. Since the information given about

Armageddon is scattered throughout Scripture, it is difficult to provide an exact interpretation of the sequence of events. The following is an attempt to put some of the pieces together in a sequential flow of events. Consider now those stages leading up to man's final war—Armageddon.

B. STAGE ONE: THE KINGS OF THE SOUTH AND NORTH INVADE ISRAEL.

Whenever the Bible refers to the north, south, east or west, it uses Palestine as the frame of reference. Therefore, the king of the North would be a great military power north of Palestine, and the king of the South would likewise refer to a military power south of Palestine.

According to *Daniel 11:40*, the king of the South, an Arab-African confederacy, launches a massive attack against Israel: "And at the end time the king of the South will collide with him...."

Along with this king of the South, another king joins the invasion—the king of the North (Russia and her allies). He makes both a land and sea assault:

"...and the king of the North will storm against him with chariots, with horsemen, and with many ships; and he will enter countries, overflow them, and pass through. He will also enter the Beautiful Land, and many countries will fall" *(Daniel 11:40,41a)*.

1. What nations will be spared during this invasion *(Daniel 11:41)*? _____

_____

_____

_____

_____
_____
_____
_____

2. What other major nation is invaded *(Daniel 11:42)*? _____
_____

Some Bible scholars believe that Egypt is double-crossed by Russia, while others believe that Egypt is not part of the southern confederacy. As the Russian commander is in Egypt, rumors from the East and North disturb him. Out of the East a massive sea of humanity marches toward Jerusalem. Out of the North another growing threat emerges *(Daniel 11:44)*. Since the Russian leader is in Egypt, the person from the North refers to someone north of Egypt—someone presently in Israel (north of Egypt). That someone is the Antichrist, who has come to Israel's defense, fulfilling his earlier peace pact.

C. STAGE TWO: RUSSIA RETURNS TO JERUSALEM AND IS ANNIHILATED.

The Russian commander quickly returns to Jerusalem to establish his headquarters: "...and he will go forth with great wrath to destroy and annihilate many. And he will pitch the tents of his royal pavilion between the seas and the beautiful Holy Mountain... *(Daniel 11:44,45a)*.

But when the Russian commander returns to Jerusalem, he is in for a surprise. Daniel says, "...yet he will come to his end, and no one will help him" *(Daniel 11:45b)*.

1. Why does Russia invade Israel *(Ezekiel 38:10-13)*? _____
_____
_____
_____

2. How will God bring the Russian army to its end *(Ezekiel 38:18-22)*? _____

3. What else will the Russian army experience *(Ezekiel 39:6)*? _____
_____
_____
_____
_____

4. How long will it take to bury the dead *(Ezekiel 39:11-16)*? _____
_____
_____
_____

The descriptions of God's judgment could refer to either direct judgment from God, as when He destroyed Sodom and Gomorrah, or it could be descriptive of nuclear warfare.

D. STAGE THREE: THE ORIENT MOVES WEST.

With the king of the South (United Arab and African armies) out of commission because of Russia and the Russian army annihilated, there are only two powers remaining: the East and the West.

The Western force under the Antichrist's control is in Jerusalem. The kings from the East begin their march toward the Holy City: "The sixth angel poured out his bowl upon the great river, the Euphrates; and its water was dried up, that the way might be prepared for the kings from the east" *(Revelation 16:12)*.

1. How many soldiers make up the army of this Eastern horde *(Revelation 9:14-16)*? _____
_____

2. What present Oriental power has this number of soldiers today? _____

While the Antichrist is in Jerusalem, he changes his peace-loving approach and takes on a new image.

1. What does this world dictator do while in Jerusalem *(2 Thessalonians 2:3,4)*? _____

_____

_____

_____

_____

2. What does the Prophet Daniel call this event *(Matthew 24:15)*? _____

_____

_____

3. What instructions does Jesus give to those living in that area when these events take place *(Matthew 24:15-21)*?

a) Those in Judea: _____

_____

_____

_____

_____

b) Him on the housetop: _____

_____

_____

_____

_____

4. How long can Jewish believers expect God's protection during this period *(Revelation 12:6,14)*?

_____

_____

_____

_____

E. STAGE FOUR: THE LEADERS OF THE WORLD FIGHT UNDER THE ANTICHRIST'S AUTHORITY AGAINST THE KINGS OF THE EAST.

According to *Revelation 16:13,14*, the Antichrist and his false prophet summon the other world leaders to obliterate the great mass of soldiers from the East. This last stage of war is fought on the Plain of Megiddo (Armageddon).

The Prophet Joel wrote about this dreadful event 27 centuries ago:

> Proclaim this among the nations: Prepare a war; rouse the mighty men! Let all the soldiers draw near, let them look up! Beat your plowshares into swords, and your pruning hooks into spears; let the weak say, "I am a mighty man." Hasten and come, all you surrounding nations, and gather yourselves there. Bring down, O Lord, Thy mighty ones. Let the nations be aroused and come up to the valley of Jehoshaphat, for there will I sit to judge all the surrounding nations. Put in the sickle, for the harvest is ripe. Come, tread, for the wine press is full; the vats overflow, for their wickedness is great. Multitudes, multitudes in the valley of decision *(Joel 3:9-14)*.

This final battle is God's judgment on sinful humanity, and it results in the worst human carnage that any battle has ever experienced. The descriptions of what takes place in and around Jerusalem as well as throughout the world are given by the Prophet Zechariah and the Apostle John.

1. Describe the events in Jerusalem at this time *(Zechariah 14:1-3)*. _____

_____

_____

_____

_____

_____

_____

2. What will happen to the armies at Armageddon *(Zechariah 14:12-15)*? _____

_____

_____

_____

_____

_____

3. As the battle is raging in the Valley of Jehoshaphat, what is taking place throughout the world *(Zechariah 14:4,5; Revelation 16:17-21)*?

_____

_____

_____

_____

_____

4. How does John describe the result of Armageddon *(Revelation 14:17-20)*? _____

_____

_____

_____

_____

_____

_____

At first glance, you would think that everyone is killed during this battle and the accompanying

worldwide earthquakes, which level cities like New York, London, Paris, Los Angeles, Tokyo, etc. However, though millions will die, some people will survive. The Prophet Zechariah predicted that two-thirds of the Jews will be destroyed, but one-third will be spared and come to know God personally:

"And it will come about in all the land," declares the Lord, "that two parts in it will be cut off and perish; but the third part will be left in it. And I will bring the third part through the fire, refine them as silver is refined, and test them as gold is tested. They will call on My name; and I will answer them; I will say, 'They are My people,' and they will say, 'The Lord is my God'" *(Zechariah 13:8,9)*.

Remember that the Bible offers only a glimpse of what will take place at Armageddon, and yet it provides enough material to sober any casual reader. The events may not occur exactly as I have described. Sequences may differ from what has been presented. But the destruction will be very real. Men will be convinced that the end of the world has come. Fear will grip the heart of every human being.

But even as life emerged through the devastating volcanic ash belched forth by Mount St. Helens, so life will emerge from the destructive forces of Armageddon. Jesus will return. The King of kings and Lord of lords will establish His kingdom on earth and place His law in the hearts of mankind. Then there will be peace to replace the terror, life to replace death, and hope to replace despair.

Graduation ceremonies are filled with mixed emotions. Tears flow because old friends will be separating and going different directions. But at the same time there is a sense of relief that it's over. You've passed! Still others sit through the ceremony nervously awaiting to see whether they will be awarded a scholarship or other special award.

Having attended numerous graduations, I have made several observations which are pertinent to our subject at hand. For example, the only people who are in the ceremony itself are the graduates. Everyone who walks up on the platform has completed his or her requirements for graduation. In addition, each graduate wears a gown to indicate that he is a candidate for graduation. Furthermore, every graduate receives some honor. It may be a diploma or it might even include a scholarship or special award of achievement. I've also observed that each graduate leaves a former lifestyle (student in high school or college) to advance toward a more productive lifestyle (high school to college or work, college to the work force, etc.). In addition, each graduate leaves his known world to advance into the world of the unknown.

What I've observed in graduation ceremonies can be related to the Bible's prediction of a super graduation day. Scriptures refer to this commencement as the judgment seat of Christ. However, before you examine what this judgment is, first understand what it is not.

A. MISCONCEPTIONS CONCERNING THE JUDGMENT SEAT OF CHRIST

1. The judgment seat does not determine who makes it to heaven.

Like the graduation ceremony, it is for graduates only. The judgment seat of Christ is for believers only.

a) How does Paul describe the believer's position *(Romans 8:1)*? _____

_____

_____

_____

b) What does Jesus say about the believer *(John 5:24)*? _____

_____

_____

_____

2. The judgment seat of Christ is not a place to punish believers for unconfessed sin.

a) How many of the believer's sins does God remember *(Hebrews 10:17)*? _____

_____

_____

b) What does John say each believer can have in the day of Christ's judgment seat *(1 John 4:17)*?

_____

_____

_____

The judgment seat of Christ is neither a determination as to who makes it to heaven nor a judgment of believers' sins. What then is this future phenomenon?

B. THE MEANING OF THE JUDGMENT SEAT OF CHRIST

The New Testament uses two words for judgment. One Greek word is *criterion*, from which our English term "criterion" is derived. The criterion is the standard by which judgment is given or the place where judgment is given. This word is used in *1 Corinthians 6:2-4* and *James 2:6*.

The second word for judgment is the Greek word *bema*. L. Sale-Harrison in his book *Judgment Seat of Christ* describes the *bema* in the following manner:

In Grecian games in Athens, the old arena contained a raised platform on which the president or umpire of the arena sat. From here he rewarded all the contestants; and here he rewarded all winners. It was called the 'bema' or 'reward seat.' It was never used of a judicial bench (p. 8).

Therefore, when the Bible refers to the judgment seat of Christ, it focuses on rewards for service rather than on punishment for sin. It is the place where Jesus Christ will honor those who have honored Him on earth. It resounds with the words, ''Well done, good and faithful servant.''

C. CHARACTERISTICS OF THE JUDGMENT SEAT OF CHRIST

The Bible refers to this event in about a dozen passages, but three major passages provide the basic teaching on this subject: *Romans 14:10-12; 1 Corinthians 3:10-15*; and *2 Corinthians 5:6-10*.

Read each passage and respond to the questions under them.

ROMANS 14:10-12

1. How should we treat fellow believers in light of the fact that we will stand before the *bema* seat?

_____

_____

_____

_____

2. How many believers will be at this *bema* seat?

_____

_____

_____

_____

1 CORINTHIANS 3:10-15

1. What metaphor is Paul using? _____

_____

_____

_____

2. What foundation is Paul referring to? _____

3. The apostle presents six kinds of building materials. But he divides them into the destructible and the indestructible. Which are which?

Destructible	Indestructible
a) _____	a) _____
_____	_____
b) _____	b) _____
_____	_____
c) _____	c) _____
_____	_____

4. Name five works that you would consider destructible. Why?

a) _____

_____

b) _____

_____

c) _____

_____

d) _____

_____

e) _____

_____

5. Name five works that you would consider indestructible. Why?

a) _____

_____

b) _____

_____

c) _____

_____

d) _____

e) _____

_____

6. Does a person lose his salvation if his works are destroyed? Explain.

_____

_____

_____

_____

_____

7. What loss would he suffer? _____

_____

_____

_____

The destructible works are primarily those which are done in the power of the flesh or with the motive of self-glory. The works themselves may be good, but if they are performed for the wrong purpose or with the wrong motive, they will perish.

| FURTHER REFERENCES |

1. What three good works does Jesus warn about doing for self-glory *(Matthew 6:2,5,16)*?

a) _____

_____

b) _____

_____

c) _____

_____

2. What other good works were being performed with a selfish motive *(Matthew 23:15,23,25,29)*?

a) _____

_____

b) _____

c) _____

_____

d) _____

_____

The indestructible works are those done in the power of God's Holy Spirit for His glory and honor. How do the following passages describe such works?

3. *1 Corinthians 10:31* — _____

_____

_____

_____

_____

4. *John 15:8* — _____

_____

_____

_____

_____

5. *Matthew 5:16* — _____

_____

_____

_____

_____

_____

Though no one knows for certain what each building material represents, several Bible commentators have suggested some possibilities. For example, Dr. John F. Walvoord has written in his book *The Church in Prophecy*, "*Wood* obviously is the best construction of the three and may represent temporary things in our life of a necessary nature as scaffolding in the construction of a building....*Hay* represents that which is more transitory, useful for animals but not fit for human consumption. *Stubble* represents that which is completely worthless. All alike, however, are reduced to ashes.

"By contrast, the gold, silver and precious stones, though much smaller in size and more difficult to obtain, are able to survive the fire. *Gold* in Scripture is typical of the glory of God and the perfection of His attributes and may represent that in our lives which is Christlike or which reveals the perfection of God's handiwork and grace. *Silver* is characteristically the metal of redemption and may speak of personal evangelism and of efforts in the extension of the Gospel. *Precious stones* are not identified and probably purposely are not related to any particular stone. This seems to refer to all other works of God manifest in the life of believers offering a great variety of beauty and color and illustrating that believers may serve the Lord in many different ways'' (p. 149).

2 CORINTHIANS 5:6-10

1. What should be the Christian's greatest ambition in life? _____

_____

_____

2. How does Paul express the purpose for the judgment seat of Christ? _____

_____

_____

_____

The words "good" or "bad" do not refer to that which is *morally* good or evil, but rather to that which is either profitable or worthless. Dr. J.

Dwight Pentecost comments, "Thus the judgment is not to determine what is ethically good or evil, but rather that which is acceptable and that which is worthless. It is not the Lord's purpose here to chasten His child for his sins, but to reward his service for those things done in the name of the Lord'' *(Things to Come*, p. 223).

SUMMARY

In this chapter you've learned that the judgment seat of Christ is somewhat like a universal graduation. This great event is for believers only, who will be arrayed in white robes to receive the honor due them. Some will experience great honor while others will be honored by the fact that they are present at the *bema* seat. Each believer has left the world of the known and passed into the world of the unknown—into the heavens.

You've further discovered that the believer is not at the *bema* seat to be convicted of past sins, but rather to be rewarded for what he has done, whether his life has demonstrated profitable or worthless works. All deeds which are motivated by fleshly interests will perish, but those motivated by godly interests will survive.

The next chapter will expand on this strategic event. You will learn about the specific rewards and the process God uses to test your works. But before you read on, pause at this moment and reflect on what you've learned and how it applies to you. Check the box which best describes you.

QUESTIONS	NUMERICAL EVALUATION				
	1 Absolutely No	2 No	3 Somewhat	4 Yes	5 Absolutely Yes
1. I look forward to the judgment seat of Christ.					
2. I expect to receive a number of heavenly awards.					
3. Most of my works should fall into the gold, silver, and precious stones category.					
4. Knowing about such a judgment seat has encouraged me to change certain areas of my life.					
5. Knowing that I'll give an account to God of my life, I plan to be less critical of other people.					

9.

Tested by Fire

Fire is a resource which produces both a blessing and a curse. It can be used for light, warmth, cooking, baking pottery, bending glass, melting metals, and other such beneficial uses. But fire has also been known to scar, maim, and destroy.

The Apostle Paul writes, "Each man's work will become evident; for the day will show it, because it is to be revealed with fire; and the fire itself will test the quality of each man's work" *(1 Corinthians 3:13)*.

The judgment seat of Christ is a period of testing by fire. The last chapter briefly mentioned works and motives, but in the following pages we will go into greater depth about what the Lord will test, what believers will do with their rewards, the type of rewards available, and how we can prevent losing our rewards.

A. WHAT WILL THE FIRE TEST?

1. The fire will test the quality of our work *(1 Corinthians 3:12,13)*.

Paul's emphasis in this passage is on work quality, not quantity: "...and the fire itself will test the *quality* of each man's work" *(1 Corinthians 3:13b)*. There are those who believe that anything we do in the name of the Lord qualifies for quality work. But much today is done in the name of the Lord or "because God led me to do it" which fails the quality test.

For example, there is a lot of church work and just plain busy work which fails the quality test. Many church boards and committees spend hours debating ecclesiastical trivia and are bogged down in maintaining the organization or denomination. They are oblivious to the crying physical and spiritual needs of the multitudes.

a) What kind of work is profitable, according to *1 Corinthians 10:24*?

_____

_____

_____

b) What kinds of works was Jesus involved with? Name ten.

(1)_____

(2)_____

(3)_____

(4)_____

(5)_____

(6)_____

(7)_____

(8)_____

(9)_____

(10)_____

c) What kind of works do many Christians and churches get bogged down in which are often worthless? Name five.

(1)_____

(2)_____

(3)_____

(4)_____

(5) _____

_____

2. The fire will test the quality of our faithfulness.

Not only is the type of work important, but the faithfulness in performing the work is vital. Many people have good intentions but never get around to beginning the work. Or they start the project and soon drop it.

Paul exhorted the believers at Corinth, "...it is required of stewards that one be found trustworthy" *(1 Corinthians 4:2)*. A steward is one who manages the affairs of another person. Since everything that we have has come from God *(1 Corinthians 4:7)*, we are to manage life with the knowledge that one day we will give an account of our stewardship.

a) How was the steward in *Luke 16:1-7* unfaithful?

_____

_____

_____

_____

b) How was the steward in *Luke 19:11-27*

   unfaithful? _____

_____

_____

_____

_____

c) In both cases how did the master respond to the

   unfaithful steward? _____

_____

_____

_____

d) List the areas of stewardship which God has given to you according to the following verses:

   (1) *1 Peter 4:10* _____

(2) *Ephesians 5:15,16* _____

_____

_____

(3) *1 Timothy 6:17-19* _____

_____

_____

_____

(4) *Romans 14:10-12* _____

_____

_____

_____

(5) *Ephesians 6:4* _____

_____

_____

(6) *1 Corinthians 9:25-27* _____

_____

_____

e) Which of these areas have you faithfully managed the best? Least?

_____

_____

3. The fire will test our motives.

The fires will not only test the believer's work and faithfulness but will also penetrate his motives. The Scriptures are quite clear that God judges the *heart* of man as well as his behavior.

"Therefore do not go on passing judgment before the time, but wait until the Lord comes, who will both bring to light the things hidden in the darkness and *disclose the motives of men's hearts*; and then

each man's praise will come to him from God"
(1 Corinthians 4:5).

When Jesus denounced the scribes and Pharisees, He did not condemn their works of giving alms, public prayer, and fasting, but rather He accused them of wrong motives—"that they may be honored by men" *(Matthew 6:2,5,16).*

In the next series of assignments, I've written the common wrong motive for serving God. Look up the corresponding references and write out the proper motive.

a) Because I have to—*obligation*

   Right motive—*1 Peter 5:2a* _____

   _____

b) Because of what I can get out of it—*greed*

   Right motive—*1 Peter 5:2b* _____

   _____

c) Because I enjoy exercising authority over others—*power*
   Right motive—*1 Peter 5:3* _____

d) Because I want people to notice me—*pride*

   Right motive—*Matthew 6:3,4,6,18* _____

   _____

e) Because I want to be liked by others—*popularity*
   Right motive—*Ephesians 6:6; Colossians*

   3:22,23 _____

f) Because I can do it without sacrifice—
   convenience

   Right motive—*1 Corinthians 9:4,11,12* _____

   _____

g) Because I can please myself—*self-gratification*

   Right motive—*1 Corinthians 10:24,33* _____

h) Because I'm jealous and want to show that I'm better than he/she—*jealousy*

   Right motive—*Philippians 1:15,16* _____

   _____

Motives play a very important role in your service for the Lord. However, there is one other aspect which will go through the scorching heat of the fires—your source of dependence.

4. The fire will test our source of dependence for our works.

Upon whom or what do you rely as you live your life? Many options are available. In the following verses list the sources from which many people seek their strength.

a) *Proverbs 3:5b* _____

   _____

b) *1 Corinthians 2:4a,5a* _____

   _____

c) *Proverbs 11:28a* _____

   _____

How is the proper source of dependence expressed in the following verses?

a) *John 15:4,5* _____

   _____

b) *Galatians 2:20* _____

   _____

c) *Galatians 5:16* _____

   _____

d) *Ephesians 5:18* _____

   _____

e) *Psalm 37:3-7*

   (1) *37:3a* _____

   _____

   (2) *37:4a* _____

   _____

   (3) *37:5a* _____

   _____

   (4) *37:7a* _____

When you serve the Lord by trusting in His power and when you are motivated to please Him, you will be a faithful manager of His affairs and will bear much fruit.

Now that you've become aware of what the fires will test, you are probably wondering what you'll do with those rewards which God will give to you for the works which have endured.

B. WHAT WILL BELIEVERS DO WITH THEIR REWARDS?

Are believers going to parade around heaven with their rewards? Will they trade them in on larger mansions and live more luxuriously than those who have few rewards? Perish the thought.

As you begin to answer this question for yourself, consider the symbols used to describe rewards:

1. What symbol does Jesus use in *Matthew 16:19-21*? _____

_____

_____

2. What word does the Lord use in *Matthew 5:12*?

_____

_____

_____

3. What terminology does Christ use in *John 4:36*?

_____

_____

_____

4. How does Paul refer to heavenly rewards in *2 Corinthians 5:10*? _____

_____

_____

5. What symbol does John use in *Revelation 3:11*?

_____

_____

_____

Whether the symbol is a crown, reward, treasure, fruit, or recompense is not as important as the fact that there are special honors awaiting those who are faithful to God and desire to please Him.

There is one indication concerning what believers will do with their rewards. As John receives the Revelation from Christ, he writes, ''The twenty-four elders will fall down before Him who sits on the throne, and will worship Him who lives forever and ever, and will *cast their crowns before the throne,* saying, 'Worthy art Thou, our Lord and our God, to receive glory and honor and power; for Thou didst create all things, and because of Thy will they existed, and were created' '' *(Revelation 4:10,11).*

Many Bible scholars believe that the 24 elders represent believers who have been rewarded but now return those rewards to God as a thank offering.

It's like going to a very special birthday party. You're so excited to attend that you forget your gift. Everyone else has a gift with which to honor their special friend, and when it's time for you to honor him, embarrassment overwhelms you, for you have nothing to offer.

Dr. J. Dwight Pentecost offers another possibility. He writes, ''From the Scriptures it is learned that the believer was redeemed in order that he might bring glory to God *(1 Corinthians 6:20)*....Inasmuch as reward is associated with brightness and shining in many passages of Scripture *(Daniel 12:3; Matthew 13:43; I Corinthians 15:40,41,49),* it may be that the reward given to the believer is a capacity to manifest the glory of Christ throughout eternity. Thus in the exercise of the reward of the believer, it will be Christ and not the believer that is glorified by the reward. Capacities to radiate the glory will differ, but there will be no personal sense of lack in that each believer will be filled to the limit of his capacity to 'show forth the praises of Him who hath called you out of darkness into His marvelous light' *(I Peter 2:9)''* *(Things to Come,* p. 226).

C. HOW CAN THE BELIEVER PREVENT THE LOSS OF REWARD?

Apparently it is possible for a Christian to lose rewards which he has already attained. Though no one else can take your rewards from you *(Matthew 6:19,20),* you yourself can lose what you have already stored up in heaven, or else you can allow someone to lead you astray and lose them in this way.

1. How does Paul say you can lose your reward *(Colossians 2:18)*? _____

_____

_____

_____

2. What does John indicate could lead to a loss of reward *(2 John 6-8)*? _____

_____

_____

_____

3. How does John warn the church of Philadelphia *(Revelation 3:11)*? _____

_____

_____

_____

You are continually laying up treasure in heaven. God has credited to your account many treasures. So here are six principles which will help you keep what is already in your account:

1. Commit yourself to win the prize *(1 Corinthians 9:24)*.

Determine in your heart that you will have something to give back to Jesus as a thank offering for everything He has done for you. Desire more than anything else to have a great capacity to honor Him throughout eternity.

2. Develop self-control in all areas of life *(1 Corinthians 9:25)*.

Paul writes, "Do you not know that those who run in a race all run, but only one receives the prize? Run in such a way that you may win. And everyone who competes in the games *exercises self-control in all things...*" *(1 Corinthians 9:24,25a)*.

According to the following passages, what are some of those categories which are included in the *all things?*

a) *1 Timothy 4:12* _____

_____

b) *1 Corinthians 9:27; 6:19,20* _____

_____

c) *2 Timothy 2:15* _____

_____

d) *1 Timothy 4:14* _____

_____

e) *1 Timothy 3:4* _____

_____

f) *1 Timothy 6:18,19* _____

_____

g) *Ephesians 6:5-9* _____

_____

3. Aim for worthwhile goals *(1 Corinthians 9:26)*.

Worthwhile goals are those which conform to the Word of God. Any of the commands in Scripture qualify as an excellent goal. List five worthwhile goals which you could set for yourself.

a) _____

_____

b) _____

_____

c) _____

_____

d) _____

_____

e) _____

_____

4. Obey the rules yourself *(1 Corinthians 9:27; 2 Timothy 2:5)*.

It is relatively easy to point out the problems in other people's lives and tell them how to change. But when it comes to living by those same rules ourselves, we like to bend them a little. We look for the exception, the loophole.

Many young people are more concerned with "How far may I go on a date?" than "How can I honor the Lord in my dating life as well as in any other area of my life?" Parents so often want their children under their authority, but want God to be a little more flexible in dealing with themselves.

5. Remove all potential hindrances from your life *(Hebrews 12:1)*.

The writer of *Hebrews* refers to "every encumbrance, and the sin which so easily entangles us." Name five problems which entangle many Christians and keep them from experiencing true freedom in Christ.

a) _____

_____

_____

b) _____

_____

_____

c) _____

_____

_____

d) _____

_____

_____

e) _____

_____

_____

6. Run the race with endurance *(Hebrews 12:1,2)*.

It's always too soon to quit. You may feel like you've had it. You may be the only one who's holding the line morally. You may be one of the only honest individuals at work. You might wonder if it's really worth living a godly life in a sin-wracked world. Well, it is. Don't give up.

a) What promise did Paul give to the person who endures *(Galatians 6:9)*? _____

_____

_____

_____

_____

_____

b) What promise does James give to those who endure *(James 1:4)*? _____

_____

_____

_____

_____

You have so much to gain, and you have an eternity to enjoy the rewards which Jesus Christ will give to those who are faithful. As you consider the judgment seat of Christ, I trust that you will anticipate that day. I pray that it will not cause you fear, but rather an emotion of excitement and hope. If it does, then you can say with the Apostle Paul, "For to me, to live is Christ, and to die is gain" *(Philippians 1:21)*.

10.

The Perfect Marriage

Time has a way of changing idealism into reality. A young couple falls madly in love with each other. From her perspective he's the perfect man, and through his eyes she's the perfect woman. They anticipate a perfect marriage, but after they say "I do," a strange phenomenon occurs. Slowly their thoughts shift from the fairy-tale ending, "they lived happily ever after," to the stark reality of "what you see is what you get."

Perfect marriages are attainable only when two perfect mates get married. And since that species died out in the Garden of Eden, such marriages must be confined to the storybooks.

However, the Bible does refer to a perfect marriage of the future, and it's no fairy tale. The ceremony will consist of a perfect bride and a perfect Groom.

1. How does Scripture characterize the bride *(Ephesians 5:25-27)*? List the bride's perfect qualities.

_____

_____

_____

_____

2. How does Scripture characterize the Groom *(1 Peter 1:18,19)*?

_____

_____

_____

_____

The marriage to which I refer is, of course, that ultimate marriage between Jesus Christ and His church. It will be perfect in beauty, love, and relationship. This marriage will know no breakdown in communication, no squabbles, no hurt feelings, no taking advantage of each other, and no divorce. It will be a marriage of mutual trust, and will last throughout eternity.

So let's search the Word of God and mine those golden nuggets of truth that will encourage us, the bride, to anticipate our Knight in shining armor, riding a white horse. "Let us rejoice and be glad and give the glory to Him, for the marriage of the Lamb has come and His bride has made herself ready.... And I saw heaven opened; and behold, a white horse and He who sat upon it is called Faithful and True; and in righteousness He judges and wages war. And His eyes are a flame of fire, and upon His head are many diadems; and He has a name written

upon Him which no one knows except Himself" *(Revelation 19:7,11,12)*.

To better understand this beautiful promise of a perfect marriage, we will focus on the marriage proclamation, personnel, peculiarities, and procedure, and we will learn how each relates to the ultimate perfect marriage.

A. THE MARRIAGE PROCLAMATION

One of the most nerve-wracking parts of organizing a wedding ceremony is to make certain that the announcements get to the right people on time. But no matter how carefully one goes through the list of invited guests, someone is usually forgotten. God wanted to make certain that the invitations would get out in plenty of time, and so He started to make the announcement over 2000 years ago.

1. Who was the first announcer of this upcoming wedding *(John 3:27-30)*? _____

2. What specifically did he announce? _____

_____

_____

3. Who was the second herald of the future wedding *(Luke 5:32-35)*? _____

_____

4. Who are the attendants of the Bridegroom? _____

_____

5. What did he say would happen to the Bridegroom?

_____

_____

6. What is the husband-and-wife relationship expected to illustrate *(Ephesians 5:28-32)*? _____

_____

The announcements are out. The Groom is preparing Himself in heaven to come for His bride. He hasn't told us when He will return, but He has given us some guideposts to help us know when the time is drawing near. Notice who will be involved in this wedding.

B. THE MARRIAGE PERSONNEL

First there is the *Bridegroom*, the Lord Jesus Christ. Paul writes of his own ministry among the Corinthians: "For I am jealous for you with a godly jealousy; for I betrothed you to one husband, that to Christ I might present you as a pure virgin" *(2 Corinthians 11:2)*.

The interesting fact about this wedding is that the main attraction is not the bride but the Bridegroom. In our culture we sing, "Here comes the bride," but the ultimate marriage will have guests singing, "Here comes the Bridegroom."

Jesus said, "Behold, I am coming quickly, and My reward is with Me, to render to every man according to what he has done....And *the Spirit* and *the bride* say, 'Come.' And let *the one who hears* say, 'Come.' And let the one who is thirsty come; let the one who wishes take the water of life without cost.... He who testifies to these things says, 'Yes, I am coming quickly.' Amen. *Come, Lord Jesus*" *(Revelation 22:12,17,20)*.

In addition to the wedding party are the invited guests, which include all true believers, and of course the Father of the Groom—God the Father.

To better understand the wedding itself, it is important to understand the customs of an Oriental rather than a Western wedding. There are four specific Biblical weddings which we'll study.

C. THE MARRIAGE PECULIARITIES

1. Adam and Eve *(Genesis 2:22-25)*

The first wedding of human history took place many years ago in a perfect setting—beautiful trees, flowers, plants, and smog-free air. As we read the *Genesis* passage, we observe three parts of the wedding: a) the bride (Eve) was chosen for the groom (Adam) by God Himself *(vv. 21,22)*; b) the bride was brought to the groom by God *(v. 22b)*; and c) the

bride and groom consummated the marriage to become one flesh *(vv. 23-25)*.

Now trace the specific aspects of the following three marriage ceremonies: (1) Isaac and Rebekah; (2) Samson; and (3) Joseph and Mary.

1. Isaac and Rebekah *(Genesis 24)*

List six different parts of the wedding from preparation to consummation.

a) *24:1-9* _____

_____

_____

b) *24:10,22,53* _____

_____

c) *24:49* (speaking to Rebekah's father, Laban)

_____

_____

_____

d) *24:51* _____

_____

e) *24:61-65* _____

_____

f) *24:66,67* _____

_____

_____

3. Samson *(Judges 14:1-10)*

List the three major aspects of this wedding.

a) *14:1-9* _____

_____

_____

b) *14:10a* _____

_____

_____

c) *14:10b* _____

_____

_____

It is interesting to notice that the wedding feast was a very special event. In Samson's case, the feast lasted for seven days *(14:12)*.

4. Joseph and Mary *(Matthew 1:18,19)*

In this account the only revealed part of the wedding plans is the betrothal period—a time when the couple was considered married but lived separately, abstaining from a sexual relationship. Note *verse 18*: ''before they came together.'' Also in *Matthew 1:25* we discover that Joseph ''kept her a virgin until she gave birth to a Son.''

These four weddings provide some idea of the special characteristics of an Oriental wedding. It's important that we visualize those particular characteristics when we read about the marriage of Christ and the church, for that wedding will follow the Oriental rather than the Occidental wedding pattern.

Now consider this future perfect marriage in all its glory and splendor. Like most Oriental weddings, it consists of three unique periods: the betrothal, the presentation, and the celebration.

D. THE MARRIAGE PROCEDURE

1. The betrothal stage

In the Near East betrothal is almost as binding as marriage. Sometimes the betrothed woman was referred to as ''wife'' *(Matthew 1:18)* and the man as ''husband'' *(Matthew 1:19)*. This betrothal included the following steps:

a) *The choice of a spouse*. Usually the parents of a young man chose his wife and arranged for the marriage *(Genesis 21:21)*. Sometimes the girl was asked whether she consented, as in the case of Rebekah *(Genesis 24:58)*. On some occasions the girl's parents chose a husband for their daughter *(Ruth 3:1,2)*.

b) *The exchange of gifts*. These types of gifts were associated with the betrothal. One was the marriage presentation. It was a compensation gift *from the bridegroom to the family of the bride,* and functioned as a seal of the covenant, binding together the two families. Another type of gift was the dowry, a gift *to the bride or the*

groom from her father (Genesis 24:53). As the betrothal period ended, the presentation period began.

2. The presentation stage

This was the public acknowledgment of the marital relationship. The bridegroom would go to the home of the bride with his friends in procession. Then he would take the bride back to his home or to his father's home for the wedding supper *(Matthew 22:1-14)*. Once the bridegroom and bride were back at the groom's father's house, the marriage was consummated and the feast began. The final period was the celebration phase.

3. The celebration

The wedding festivities usually continued for an entire week *(Genesis 29:27)* or longer. They included feasting, music, and various kinds of entertainment.

Each of these Oriental wedding periods corresponds precisely with the marriage between Christ and His church.

E. The MARRIAGE OF CHRIST AND HIS CHURCH

1. The betrothal period

a) The choice of a spouse *(Ephesians 1:3,4)*

(1) Who made the choice of a bride? _____

_____

(2) When was the choice made? _____

_____

(3) What is the purpose behind that choice?

_____

_____

_____

(4) How else is this purpose described in

2 Thessalonians 2:13? _____

_____

_____

_____

_____

b) The dowry payment *(1 Corinthians 6:19,20; 1 Peter 1:18,19)*

   (1) Who paid the dowry price? _____

      _____

   (2) What was the price? _____

      _____

c) The gift to the bride

Today the groom gives the bride-to-be an engagement ring. It is his pledge to fulfill his promise of marriage. The Greek term translated ''pledge'' is used in classical Greek for an engagement ring.

   (1) What engagement ring did Christ give to His bride *(2 Corinthians 1:22; Ephesians 1:13,14)*? _____

      _____

      _____

      _____

   (2) What was the qualification to receive the engagement ring *(Ephesians 1:13)*?

      _____

      _____

      _____

      _____

Today you are enjoying this betrothal period. The Groom is in heaven. You, the bride, continue to remain in your home, awaiting the fulfillment of a special promise.

Write out the promise of the Bridegroom before He went to His Father's house *(John 14:2,3)*.

_____

_____

_____

_____

_____

_____

_____

2. The presentation period

The Groom comes for His bride *(1 Thessalonians 4:15-17; 1 Corinthians 15:51,52)*

a) What musical instrument accompanies the Groom? _____

      _____

      _____

b) Where will the bride meet the Groom? _____

      _____

      _____

c) How long will the bride remain with her Groom? _____

      _____

Following the processional to the Groom's Father's house, the scene is set for the actual wedding. After the marriage ceremony the third stage of the wedding begins.

3. The celebration period

Jesus spoke about a king who gave a wedding feast for his son. As the preparations were being made, he sent his servants to inform the invited guests that the wedding feast was ready *(Matthew 22:1-14)*.

a) How did the invited guests respond to the announcement? _____

      _____

b) How did the king respond to their lack of cooperation? _____

      _____

      _____

c) What was the threefold response of the invited guests to this second announcement?

   (1) _____

      _____

      _____

   (2) _____

_____

_____

(3) _____

_____

_____

d) Did the king give a third announcement to these invited guests? _____

_____

e) Who then was invited to share the feast? _____

_____

_____

f) To what degree was it important to be wearing wedding clothes? _____

_____

_____

_____

This account gives you some idea as to how important it was for the invited guests to participate in the wedding banquet, and that they wear the proper attire. If anyone attempted to crash the party without the proper attire, he would be thrown out. This parable should help you better understand the significance of the marriage feast. Dr. J. Dwight Pentecost makes a distinction between the marriage of the Lamb and the marriage supper. He writes, "The marriage of the Lamb is an event that has particular reference to the church and takes place in heaven. The marriage supper is an event that involved Israel and takes place on the earth. The wedding supper, then, becomes the parabolic picture of the entire millennial age, to which Israel will be invited during the tribulation period, which invitation *many will reject*, and so they will be cast out, and *many will accept* and they will be received in. Because of the rejection the invitation will likewise go to the Gentiles so that many of them will be included. Israel, at the second advent, will be waiting for the Bridegroom to come from the wedding ceremony and invite them to that supper, at which the Bridegroom will introduce His bride to His friends *(Matthew 25:1-13)*" (*Things to Come*, pp. 227-28).

Follow the coming of the bride and Groom after the ceremony in *Revelation 19:1-10*.

a) What clothes does the bride wear? _____

_____

_____

_____

b) What do they symbolize? _____

_____

_____

_____

Do you see the importance of both the bride and guests wearing the right clothes *(Revelation 19:14)*?

At this point the bride moves into a new circle of friends and acquaintances. She greets the guests who have come to the banquet supper and enjoys not only the festivities of the banquet, but also the presence of her Groom.

The church will enjoy a banquet which will last not a week, a month, or even a year, but rather 1000 years. If you have been bought with Christ's blood, you will enjoy that feast not only with those believers who make up the church, but with the saints of all ages.

11

The Reign of Christ

The Prophet Isaiah described the Messiah's first coming to earth as one of sorrow and rejection: "He was despised and forsaken of men, a man of sorrows, and acquainted with grief; and like one from whom men hide their face, He was despised, and we did not esteem Him....He was oppressed and He was afflicted, yet He did not open His mouth; like a lamb that is led to slaughter, and like a sheep that is silent before its shearers, so He did not open His mouth" *(Isaiah 53:3,7).*

But when Jesus returns the second time to earth, He will not be the lowly Lamb. He will come as the Lion of Judah, the King of Kings and Lord of Lords. He will not come to be judged by the puny mind of man, but will Himself judge the world in righteousness and justice.

So prepare yourself to study an event that will accomplish what no nation or ruler has ever been able to achieve — peace on earth.

This chapter will lead you through the various events which unfold as Jesus returns to earth, the individuals who will populate the world when Christ returns, the characteristics of Jesus' reign, and the events following His kingly rule.

A. THE UNFOLDING EVENTS OF CHRIST'S RETURN TO EARTH

World chaos sets the scene for Jesus' return. The judgments of God have been poured out on mankind *(Revelation chapters 6—18).* The Antichrist is in power and the nations of the world are gathered at Armageddon to fight against one another. The great cities of the world have been demolished by the greatest earthquake this earth has ever experienced. Hundred-pound hailstones have pelted the landscape, killing millions of people. Suddenly all eyes look upward: "Immediately after the tribulation of those days, the sun will be darkened, and the moon will not give its light, and the stars will fall from the sky, and the powers of the heavens will be shaken, and *then the sign of the Son of Man will appear in the sky*, and then all the tribes of the earth will mourn, and they will see the Son of Man coming on the clouds of the sky with power and great glory" *(Matthew 24:29,30).*

It is an effect similar to the feelings of two brothers fighting each other in the darkness of their bedroom. Suddenly the door swings open, the lights flash on, and there in the doorway stands Dad with anger written all over his face.

There will be no place to run or hide. No escape. Man is about to face his eternal Judge, who knows the very hearts of mankind.

1. Five names are given to the Lord as He returns to judge man. What are those names *(Revelation 19:11-21)*?

a) _____

_____

b) _____

_____

c) _____

_____

d) _____

_____

e) _____

_____

2. How does the passage describe His purpose in coming back to earth? _____

_____

_____

_____

_____

3. How will Jesus rule over the earth? What do you think this means? _____

_____

_____

_____

4. What action do the armies take which were fighting one another? _____

_____

_____

5. What happens to the beast and false prophet?

_____

_____

_____

_____

6. When Jesus returns, where will He touch down (*Acts 1:9-12; Zechariah 14:4*)? _____

_____

_____

_____

7. What geological changes will occur at that time (*Zechariah 14:4,5*)? _____

_____

_____

_____

_____

8. What will happen to Satan during the period in which Christ reigns on earth (*Revelation 20:1-3*)?

_____

_____

_____

_____

Now the earth is prepared for the Lord to reign. Sin has been judged. Those who rebelled against God are dead. The beast and false prophet are in the lake of fire, and Satan is bound for 1000 years. But who will be reigning with Christ? Who will populate the earth?

B. THE PARTICIPANTS IN THE THOUSAND-YEAR REIGN WITH CHRIST

There will be two groups of people who participate in the millennial (thousand-year) kingdom. One group will enter with their normal physical bodies and populate the kingdom while the second group will enter with their new bodies and reign with Christ. Those who populate the earth with natural bodies will include Jewish and Gentile believers who came into a personal relationship with Christ during the tribulation period. The life of Jewish believers during the millennial reign of Christ is recorded in *Isaiah 65*, and the Gentiles in *Matthew 25:31-46*. Those who will have new bodies include the church (Christ's bride), the resurrected tribulation believers, and the Old Testament saints.

1. What two groups of church saints will reign with Christ?

1) *1 Thessalonians 4:13-16* _____

_____

_____

b) *1 Thessalonians 4:17* _____

_____

_____

2. What threefold description is given concerning the tribulation saints (*Revelation 20:4*)? _____

_____

_____

_____

_____

3. How did the Old Testament believer Job express his assurance of living with his Redeemer (*Job 19:25,26*)? _____

_____

_____

_____

_____

_____

C. THE RELATIONSHIP BETWEEN BELIEVERS WITH NATURAL BODIES AND THOSE WITH RESURRECTED BODIES

You may be wondering how the people with earthly physical bodies and those with resurrected bodies will be able to live together on earth. Though this phenomenon seems strange, two precedents already exist for such cohabitation. One such precedent is the existence of angels and mankind at present. Angels do not have homes or marry or procreate. Yet they are very much alive and active.

1. In the following passages list some of the ministries which angels have.

a) *Matthew 4:6* _____

_____

_____

b) *Genesis 24:7* _____

_____

_____

c) *1 Kings 19:5-8* _____

_____

_____

d) *Matthew 1:20-24* _____

_____

_____

e) *Acts 8:26* _____

_____

_____

f) *Acts 12:20-23* _____

_____

_____

g) *Hebrews 13:2* _____

_____

_____

h) *Luke 16:22* _____

_____

_____

2. What future ministry does the Lord give to angels (*Matthew 13:41,42*)?

The second illustration of resurrected and non-resurrected people communicating together is the period when Jesus walked this earth for 50 days in His newly acquired body. List several characteristics of Jesus' resurrected body. What could it do? What could others see?

a) *John 20:20* _____

_____

_____

b) *John 20:26* _____

_____

_____

c) *John 20:27* _____

_____

_____

d) *John 21:13* _____

_____

_____

e) *Acts 1:9-11* _____

_____

_____

The relationship between those who have not died and those who have their resurrected bodies should not be any more strange than the relationship between the resurrected Christ and His disciples. They talked with one another, ate and drank together, and made plans for the future.

So far you've seen the setting for Christ to return, and have learned about those who will populate the kingdom and how they relate with each other. Now prepare to look into the future and learn about the kind of world that God meant for us to live in.

D. THE NATURE OF CHRIST'S KINGDOM

The Scriptures exquisitely describe life during the thousand-year reign of Christ. Look up the following references and write a description of the millennial kingdom.

1. *Isaiah 65:20* _____
_____
_____
_____

2. *Isaiah 11:6-9; 65:25* _____
_____
_____
_____

3. *Micah 4:3* _____
_____
_____
_____

4. *Isaiah 11:4* _____
_____
_____
_____

5. *Micah 4:2* _____
_____
_____
_____

6. *Isaiah 33:24; 35:5* _____
_____
_____
_____

7. *Isaiah 65:21,22* _____
_____
_____
_____
_____

8. *Zechariah 14:16,20,21* _____
_____
_____
_____

9. *Zechariah 14:17-19* _____
_____
_____
_____

10. *Ezekiel 34:25-30* _____
_____
_____
_____

Can you imagine that kind of lifestyle where people will be at peace with one another? No one will need to live in poverty, hunger, and filth. No sickness, no early death. And all the nations will want to go to Jerusalem, not as a tourist of the Middle East, but as a worshiper of Jesus Christ.

Though this may sound like someone's overactive imagination, it is nevertheless a reality of the future—a reality that you will experience on the condition that Jesus lives in you already.

Signs of Christ's Return

Though I'm a native Pennsylvanian, my ministry and family life have been planted in Fresno, California. The rich soil of this beautiful San Joaquin Valley has made Fresno County the number one agribusiness in the United States. One of my first discoveries about this central California agricultural paradise was that, along with cotton, almonds, citrus fruit, peaches, plums, and nectarines, it also produces a variety of Biblical trees, such as the palm, sycamore, olive, myrtle, and fig tree.

Being from the East, I was used to seeing maple, oak, elm, walnut, and chestnut trees. But when I first laid eyes on a fig tree, I knew I was gazing on a unique creation of God. When the winter fog covers the valley, you experience an eerie sight if you walk through a fig orchard. The landscape looks like a scene from a Frankenstein movie. The trees themselves are twisted and gnarled, shooting forth twisting branches. You almost expect some monster to come lunging out from behind one of the trees. But when spring arrives, the barren eeriness transforms into a sight of beauty. First come the blossoms, followed by the leaves. And when the leaves sprout, you know that the hot summer days are just around the corner.

Jesus used the fig tree as an illustration several times in His ministry. On one occasion He cursed a fig tree which had produced leaves but no fruit *(Matthew 21:19)*. Later Jesus used the fig tree in a parable. He said, "Now learn the parable from the fig tree: when its branch has already become tender, and puts forth its leaves, you know that summer is near; even so you too, when you see all these things, recognize that He is near, right at the door. Truly I say to you, this generation will not pass away until all these things take place" *(Matthew 24:32-34)*.

The parable focuses on the second coming of Christ. Though no one will know the day or the hour when He will return, Jesus does provide a number of signs. The significant phrase is "when you see all these things."

The "things" to which Jesus referred are found in *Matthew 24*. Jesus' disciples had responded to His remarks about the destruction of the temple by asking, "Tell us, when will these things be, and what will be the sign of Your coming, and of the end of the age?" *(Matthew 24:3)*.

The Lord replies by answering the last question first—the end of the age *(24:4-14)*. The age of which He is speaking included the period in which He and His disciples were living. That period would extend to the end of the tribulation *(Matthew 24:4-20)*. Then Jesus answered the first question—"What will be the sign of Your coming?" In *Matthew 20:30* He states, "And then the sign of the Son of Man will appear in the sky, and then all the tribes of the earth will mourn, and they will see the Son of Man coming on the clouds of the sky with power and great glory."

This event takes place immediately after the tribulation of those days *(Matthew 24:29)*. Therefore the end of the age is actually the end of the tribulation, before the sign of the Son of Man appears in the sky.

But what are those specific events which are to occur before the great tribulation, which begins with the Antichrist setting himself up to be worshiped in Jerusalem, thus fulfilling Daniel's prophecy *(Matthew 24:15,21)*? I have found in this passage seven major characteristics of the age preceding the great tribulation, followed by the second coming of Christ.

The first major characteristic of the latter days is a proliferation of false messiahs. "And Jesus answered and said to them, 'See to it that no one misleads you. For many will come in My name, saying, "I am the Christ," and will mislead many'" *(Matthew 24:4,5)*.

A. A PROLIFERATION OF FALSE MESSIAHS

Along with Jesus' prediction concerning the spiritual atmosphere of the last days, John also warns, "Beloved, do not believe every spirit, but test the spirits to see whether they are from God; because many false prophets have gone out into the world" *(1 John 4:1)*. Likewise, the Apostle Paul warned, "But the Spirit explicitly says that in later times some will fall away from the faith, paying attention to deceitful spirits and doctrines of demons" *(1 Timothy 4:1)*.

The past 20 years have witnessed a tremendous increase of interest in witchcraft, psychic phenomena, the occult, and astrology. Eastern religions have driven a powerful wedge into the Western mind. Such ideas and philosophies at one time were considered weird by most Western minds, but today thousands of people who should know better are embracing the teachings of various gurus as though they were truth personified.

The doctrines of demons are entering the minds of millions of youth as they abandon themselves to the music of the rock stars. And who could forget the Guyana tragedy, in which a self-proclaimed messiah led over 900 totally dedicated followers to mass suicide?

The false messiahs are increasing. Their doctrines appear in various forms, including religious cults, self-awareness groups, drugs, and music.

1. What test does John give to distinguish between true doctrine and false doctrine *(1 John 2:22)*?

_____

_____

_____

_____

_____

2. What is the significance of someone denying the Son *(1 John 2:23)*? _____

_____

_____

3. What other test does John give to determine what is the truth *(1 John 4:2,3)*? _____

_____

_____

_____

_____

4. What does it mean when someone believes that Jesus is the Christ (the Messiah) *(1 John 5:1)*?

_____

_____

_____

_____

Besides the proliferation of false messiahs, Jesus warns of another growing problem which will characterize the last days: "And you will be hearing of wars and rumors of wars; see that you are not frightened, for those things must take place, but *that is not yet the end*. For nation will rise against nation, and kingdom against kingdom…" *(Matthew 24:6,7a)*.

B. WARS AND RUMORS OF WARS *(Matthew 24:6)*

War has always been a part of the human race, but at no other time in history has man had the capacity to totally destroy himself. Our generation is on a collision course of a nuclear holocaust. The U.S. has enough nuclear warheads stored in underground silos, on nuclear submarines, and in sophisticated jets around the world to launch an all-out attack which would kill every man, woman, and child in the world 12 times over! If a total nuclear war broke out, between 95 and 120 million Americans could die immediately, with millions of others dying in the weeks following (Jeremy Rifkin, *The Emerging Order*, p. 267).

According to the International Atomic Energy Agency, there are some 340 research reactors and 475 power reactors in operation or under construction in a total of 46 nations. The agency's deputy director, Hans Grumm, stated, "Any really determined nation could now produce the bomb" (*Time* Magazine, June 22, 1981, p. 40).

Today the countries which have already exploded the bomb or have the bomb include the U.S., U.S.S.R., China, France, India, and most likely Israel. Iraq was building its reactor until eight Israeli F-16 bombers escorted by six F-15's released their payload near Baghdad. Within minutes, Iraq's 260-million-dollar research reactor lay demolished.

Add to these statistics a weapons program which the U.S. has launched to catch up with Russia, and you will understand that wars and rumors of wars will further escalate.

According to *U.S. News & World Report*, "Vast improvements in the accuracy and power of Soviet missiles could give the Kremlin the means—at least in theory—to wipe out all 1,054 of America's land-based missiles in a first strike. That, according to one recent defense survey, could confront an American President with 'a choice between sur-render and Armageddon'" (*U.S. News*, February 16, 1981, p. 34). The following chart shows why the U.S. is determined to expand its military power. This chart is taken from *U.S. News*, February 16, 1981.

	U.S.	U.S.S.R.
1. Soldiers	963,000	1.8 million
2. Tanks	12,875	50,000
3. Aircraft	5,316	5,775
4. Missiles and bombers	2,058	2,582
5. Total warheads	9,000	7,000
6. Estimated megaton of warheads	3,300	5,500
7. Ships	460	800
8. Attack submarines	81	257

Though the chart focuses on the superpowers, wars and rumors of wars continue to proliferate in South Africa, Afghanistan, the Middle East, Ireland, Latin America, and just about every other country in the world.

1. Since the Bible predicts that wars will increase, is it important to work toward peace? Why?

_____

_____

_____

_____

_____

_____

_____

2. What is the origin of war, according to *James 4:1*? _____

_____

3. What, therefore, is the only lasting solution to war *(Matthew 15:18-20)*? _____

_____

_____

_____

4. How can man have peace in the midst of turmoil and war?

a) *Isaiah 26:3* _____

_____

_____

_____

b) *Romans 5:1* _____

_____

_____

c) *Philippians 4:4-7* _____

_____

_____

_____

A third characteristic of the end times will include famines: "and in various places there will be famines…" *(Matthew 24:7).*

C. FAMINES IN VARIOUS PLACES
(Matthew 24:6,7)

In many parts of the world, famine and starvation are a way of life. It is estimated that 800 million people are going hungry every day. Fifteen to twenty million Third World deaths annually—three-fourths of them children—result directly from malnutrition. Twenty-eight people are dying throughout the world each minute as a result of hunger. Eighty percent of the world's population, mostly living in villages, have no system of health care (Jeremy Rifkin, *Entropy*, p. 189).

One of the major problems which the world needs to grapple with is food distribution. The United States has been blessed by God with a tremendous wealth of natural resources. But few countries of the world experience such bounty.

According to a United Nations report, 1800 calories daily are minimum for subsistence. Yet in the hungry world half of the people live on 1900 calories daily, while the other half live on only 1000 calories daily.

In contrast, the affluent world population consumes four pounds of food daily, which comes out to 3200 calories.

Some world leaders fear that the next war will not be fought over oil, but rather over food. How long will the "have not" nations continue to put up without the basic necessities of life? There are those who have concern over the possibility of being blackmailed by a nation which has the bomb along with millions of starving people. Would a nation such as India ever come to that point where it says, "Give us food or else?"

For Americans who spend millions of dollars annually trying to take off the ugly fat, it's difficult to grasp hunger. To us, hunger is going to bed without a snack at night. For much of the world, hunger is a way of life and death.

1. Have you or your church done anything recently to deal with world famine? Explain. _____

_____

_____

_____

_____

2. What was the Old Testament attitude toward the poor and hungry *(Deuteronomy 15:7-11)*? _____

_____

_____

3. What was Jesus' attitude toward the poor *(Matthew 15:32)*? _____

_____

_____

4. What could you do to help the poor and hungry in your city? _____

_____

_____

_____

_____

5. What could you do to help the millions who starve annually in the Third World nations? _____

_____

_____

_____

_____

_____

13.

More Signs of Christ's Return

You've already learned that the Lord had predicted specific future events to serve as indicators pointing to His second coming. They include a proliferation of false messiahs, wars and rumors of wars, and famines in various parts of the world.

In this chapter you'll observe four other such signs, including earthquakes, persecution, lawlessness, and worldwide preaching of the Gospel.

Jesus said, "...and in various places there will be famines and earthquakes. But all these things are merely the beginning of birth pangs" *(Matthew 24:7,8)*.

A. EARTHQUAKES

Because I live in California, earthquakes have become very real to me. According to all the geological maps, the San Joaquin Valley is supposedly one of the safest places to live in all of California. I tried to remember that when I attempted to sleep in a bed that was shaking one Saturday evening, only to be followed by a similar experience the very next Saturday evening. I again attempted to comfort my mind with those "facts" as I preached to a packed congregation in my Fresno church as the entire building shook and rumbled, and the balcony swayed like a wave in the sea.

Earthquakes certainly aren't new to the twentieth century. The Bible speaks of earthquakes in the Old Testament *(1 Kings 19:11; Zechariah 14:4,5)*. Paul and Silas sang in a Philippian jail during an earthquake *(Acts 16:25,26)*. There have always been earthquakes as our planet has reeled from within, dispersing enormous amounts of pressure as one giant plate pushed against another. But what is different today is the increased regularity and intensity of earthquakes. In our generation these convulsions of Planet Earth have become more numerous and more deadly. Dr. John Wesley White estimates that over the past six centuries earthquakes have increased by 2189 percent (John Wesley White, *WW III*, p. 48).

In 1976 alone there were one million measurable quakes. Six of these measured 7 or more on the Richter Scale as they shook China. Today geological experts no longer talk about *if* California will experience a major earthquake but *when*.

The *Book of Revelation* unveils this dreadful future scene: "And there were flashes of lightning and sounds and peals of thunder; and there was a great earthquake, such as there had not been since man came to be upon the earth, so great an earthquake was it, and so mighty. And the great city was split into three parts, and *the cities of the nations fell...*" *(Revelation 16:18,19)*. Earthquakes are terrifying experiences, but as we look at the next characteristic of the last days, it's even more terrifying.

B. PERSECUTION OF BELIEVERS

Jesus warned, "Then they will deliver you to tribulation and will kill you, and you will be hated by all nations on account of My name" *(Matthew 24:9)*. At first reading of these verses one might be tempted to interpret this as referring to the nation of Israel. And it is true that for centuries the Jew has been persecuted. Hitler exterminated over six million Jews; Russia has killed about as many; the Arabs vow to remove Israel from the face of the earth. In fact, the United States is about the only friend which Israel has left.

However, notice the sentence: "and you shall be hated by all nations on account of *My name*." Jesus is speaking here, but today Jews are not persecuted because of Jesus' name. *Christians* are persecuted because of His name. Today in many parts of the world believers are imprisoned, tortured, and executed because they will not deny the Lord who bought them.

According to the Apostle John, in the latter days before Jesus comes, tribulation saints will experience a worldwide persecution: "And when He broke the fifth seal, I saw underneath the altar the souls of those who had been slain because of the word of God, and because of the testimony which they had maintained; and they cried out with a loud voice, saying, 'How long, O Lord, holy and true, wilt Thou refrain from judging and avenging our blood on those who dwell on the earth?' And there was given to each of them a white robe; and they were told that they should rest for a little while longer, until the number of their fellow servants and their brethren who were to be killed even as they had been, should be completed also'' *(Revelation 6:9-11)*. ''After these things I looked, and behold, a great multitude, which no one could count, from *every nation* and *all tribes* and *peoples* and *tongues,* standing before the throne and before the Lamb, clothed in white robes, and palm branches were in their hands....And one of the elders answered, saying to me, 'These who are clothed in the white robes, who are they, and from where have they come?' And I said to him, 'My lord, you know.' And he said to me, 'These are the ones who come out of the great tribulation, and they have washed their robes and made them white in the blood of the Lamb'' *(Revelation 7:9,13,14)*.

Today thousands of church saints are being persecuted throughout the world. Once the Restrainer, the Holy Spirit, is removed from the ministry of restraining sin throughout the earth *(2 Thessalonians 2:6-8)*, the Antichrist will have his revenge on believers living during the tribulation. And he will decree that they be put to death *(Revelation 13:7)*.

1. What did Jesus say about persecution *(John 15:20)*? _____

_____

_____

_____

2. What did Jesus promise His disciples for their future *(John 16:33)*? _____

_____

_____

_____

3. How did various Christian Jews attempt to escape persecution *(Galatians 6:12)*? _____

_____

_____

_____

4. Who will be the most persecuted *(2 Timothy 3:12)*? _____

_____

_____

_____

5. What do you think some Christians will do in order to escape persecution? _____

_____

_____

_____

_____

_____

Billy Graham sees this period in which Christians in the United States experience little persecution as subnormal. He writes, ''We have no scriptural foundation for believing that we can forever escape being physically persecuted for Christ's sake. The fact that we are not being persecuted is an abnormal condition. The normal condition for Christians is that they should suffer persecution *(Till Armageddon*, p. 172).

Then Graham mentions various ways by which we can prepare for inevitable suffering and persecution (pp. 173-81):

1. We should make sure of our relationship to God.
2. We should learn now to walk with God in our daily life.
3. We need to fortify ourselves with the Word.
4. We need to fortify ourselves with prayer.
5. We must fortify ourselves by realizing the nearness of the Lord at all times.
6. We need to foster and strengthen the small group movement, the concept of ''Christian cells.'' This should begin in the family.

A sixth sign to observe for the fast-approaching return of Christ is the growing lawlessness throughout the world.

C. LAWLESSNESS

Jesus predicted, "And because lawlessness is increased, most people's love will grow cold" *(Matthew 24:12)*. Has lawlessness increased recently? Of course it has.

Today we are experiencing worldwide terrorism on an unprecedented scale. A group of terrorists held 52 American diplomats hostage for 444 days, disregarding all international law. Six months after the hostage release, a bomb ripped through the headquarters of the Islamic Republican Party in Tehran, killing 72 people, including four government ministers, six deputy ministers, 20 members of Parliament, and Beheshti, the second-most-powerful man in Iran. In the United States a would-be assassin fired five times at President Reagan, wounding four men, including the President. A short time later in Vatican Square, Italy, another would-be assassin fired at the Pope, wounding the Pontiff and two bystanders. Offenses of all types rose by 10 percent in the United States from 1979 to 1980, and violent crimes jumped by 13 percent. Robberies increased by 20 percent, rape by 8 percent, aggravated assault by 8 percent, and murder by 7 percent. Among property crimes, burglary showed a rise of 14 percent and larceny 8 percent *(U.S. News*, July 13, 1981, p. 53).

This nation has become a nation of people who are beginning to fight back. Individuals are spending millions of dollars on tear-gas classes and equipment. Others are taking judo and karate classes. Other millions are buying guns, and many of them are taking training classes on how to use them for protection. Neighborhood patrols are being focused around the country to protect local residences. Worried property owners are purchasing television monitors, electronic alarms, and panic buttons to alert police. Many wealthy people are hiring guards to watch over their property. "Nationwide sales of residential burglar alarms rose from 83 million dollars in 1976 to 142 million in 1980, with sales forecast to reach 240 million by 1984" *(U.S. News,* July 13, 1981, p. 55).

Paul warned Timothy about lawlessness when he wrote his second letter: "But realize this, that in the last days difficult times will come" *(2 Timothy 3:1-5)*.

1. List the 19 charateristics of the last days' lawless society.

a) _____

b) _____

c) _____

d) _____

e) _____

f) _____

g) _____

h) _____

i) _____

j) _____

k) _____

l) _____

m) _____

n) _____

o) _____

p) _____

q) _____

r) _____

s) _____

2. Choose three of these characteristics and illustrate them with recent events.

a) _____

_____

_____

_____

_____

b) _____

_____

_____

_____

c) _____
_____
_____
_____
_____
_____
_____
_____

The final characteristic to observe before the Lord returns is the focus on the gospel explosion.

D. PREACHING OF THE GOSPEL THROUGHOUT THE WORLD

Jesus concluded His remarks about the nature of the last days by saying, "And this gospel of the kingdom shall be preached in the whole world for a witness to all the nations, and *then the end shall come*" *(Matthew 24:14)*. Preceding the end of the age is the worldwide preaching of the gospel. Some interpret this to be different from the preaching of the gospel of Christ crucified, dead, and risen. (This is referred to as the gospel of grace.) But the gospel that Matthew predicted is called the gospel of the kingdom—the same gospel that John the Baptist preached and Jesus Himself preached: "Repent, for the kingdom of heaven is at hand" *(Matthew 3:2)*; "From that time Jesus began to preach and say, 'Repent, for the kingdom of heaven is at hand'" *(Matthew 4:17)*.

A "gospel" is "good news." To those who were looking for the prophesied Messiah to come, it was good news that the King was offering His kingdom. Likewise, to those going through the tribulation, they will hear the good news of the coming kingdom preached to them. This gospel, I believe, not only includes the news of the coming King, but also the news of the crucified, risen, and ascended coming King. I believe the best interpretation of this passage is to pinpoint that preaching during the tribulation period. As the gospel goes out to the world through the 144,000 evangelists *(Revelation chapters 17 and 14)*, many people will place their faith in Jesus Christ as Savior, Lord, and coming Messiah.

However, I believe we are witnessing the beginning of this prophetic statement. The Bible has gone out to the nations of the world in their own languages. In fact, it is estimated that the Scriptures have now been published in languages spoken by 97 percent of the world. In Indonesia and South Korea, the rate of evangelical expansion is four times the population growth. In South America, evangelicals are growing at the rate of 15 percent per year, and Africa's evangelical expansion is even greater south of the Sahara.

With satellites in the air, Christian television and radio programs are beamed around the world. In his book *The Emerging Order*, Jeremy Rifkin comments, "Now, for the first time, the major TV and radio networks and their commercial sponsors are being directly challenged by a powerful new communications force. Its programming philosophy is to spread the good word of Christ. Its sponsors are tens of millions of born-again Christians. Its market audience is the planet earth. Its advertising goal is to bring three billion human beings to Christ between now and the millennium in the year A.D. 2000. Today, 1300 radio stations—one out of every seven in America—is Christian-owned and operated. Every seven days a new Christian-owned radio station is established. Together, these stations reach a listening audience of 150 million people. At the same time, Christian broadcasters are adding one new owned and operated television station to their arsenal every thirty days" (p. 105).

It is also interesting to note that the three major contenders for the U.S. Presidency in 1980 were self-acclaimed born-again Christians (Reagan, Carter, and Anderson).

The gospel of Jesus Christ is penetrating the world as never before. I believe that this is just a foretaste of the time when the gospel of the kingdom will be preached worldwide and will prepare the way for the King of Kings and Lord of Lords to touch down at Mount Olivet, splitting the mountain in two.

Yes, fig leaves are an excellent sign that summer is near. And the fig leaves of prophecy point to the fact that Jesus is coming soon. However, there are other signs not mentioned in *Matthew 24:3-14*. Therefore, read the following passages and write out what you think those other signs may be.

1. *Luke 17:26-30* _____

2. *Ezekiel 36:22-28* _____

3. *Ezekiel 38:14-16; 39:1-6* _____

4. *Daniel 2:40-43; Revelation 17:12* _____

5. *2 Thessalonians 2:3* _____

6. *1 Timothy 4:1,2* _____

7. *2 Peter 3:3,4* _____

8. *Daniel 12:4* _____

9. *Acts 2:18-20* _____

10. *Revelation 11:1* _____

11. *Revelation 11:9* _____

12. *Revelation 9:16; 16:12* _____

_____

Some of these references provide exact statements about future events. Other references *imply* what might occur. So check your answers with those given at the bottom of the page, and see whether you agree with the conclusions and inferences.

Although many of the characteristics mentioned in this chapter can be traced throughout man's history, at no other time has there been such an acceleration of so many events in one generation.

I was born in 1937, when few of these characteristics existed. In fact, the majority of these signs became most evident after World War Two. Jesus said, ''...When you see all these things, recognize that He is near, right at the door.... Therefore be on the alert, for you do not know which day your Lord is coming'' *(Matthew 24:33,42).*

The day and the hour are hidden from man, but *the generation* in which all these events take place is clearly revealed: ''Truly I say to you, this generation will not pass away until all these things take place'' *(Matthew 24:34).* I believe that we are living in that generation.

1. Business as usual.
2. Israel restored as nation to Palestine, 1948.
3. Rise of Russia as world power.
4. Ten-nation confederacy—European Common Market (United States of Europe).
5. Apostasy (falling away from truth).
6. Increase in demonic activity.
7. Skeptics concerning second coming.
8. Knowledge explosion (knowledge now doubles every 2½ years).
9. Possible nuclear warfare.
10. Rebuilt temple.
11. Possible hint of satellite TV.
12. An army of 200 million—Red China already has that.

14.

Time Sequence

You have completed a firsthand study of Bible prophecy and are now aware of present signs pointing toward future events. The concepts of the Antichrist, the rapture, the tribulation, and the judgment seat of Christ are familiar to you. But the total picture remains incomplete. You have all the pieces of the prophetic puzzle, but they have not been placed in any specific chronological order.

You may be a premillennialist, a postmillennialist, or an amillennialist. If you are premillennial, you could be a pretribulationist, a midtribulationist, a posttribulationist, or a partial-rapturist. On the other hand, you may not have the slightest idea of what any of those terms mean, and couldn't care less. Well, I believe that what you believe about prophetic chronology is important, as well as why you believe it.

Therefore, this chapter will provide a panorama of the prevalent views concerning the time sequence of future events. Since volumes could be written in defense of one position or another, I've chosen not to elaborate on each viewpoint, but instead I will provide the major views of time sequences, and then I will share which view I feel most comfortable with and why I hold that particular view. I do not ridicule any other concept. If a brother or sister has studied the Scriptures carefully and yet differs from my understanding or sequence, I accept their best effort with no sense of judgment. I also would expect you, the reader, to allow me the same honest effort along with its human limitations.

So let's look at the major views concerning the millennial reign of Christ, and then consider the differing ideas about when the rapture will occur.

A. AMILLENNIALISM

The amillennialist does not believe in a literal thousand-year reign of Christ. The prefix "a" before millennium means "no" millennium. Adherents of amillennialism believe that at present there exist both the kingdom of God and the kingdom of Satan, which will continue until the second coming of Christ.

If this view were drawn on a time chart, it would look something like this:

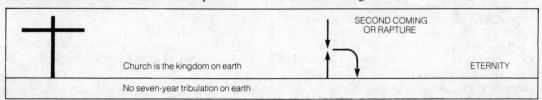

Another variation of amillennialism would look at the future in the following way:

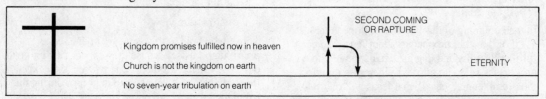

In his book entitled *The Millennium*, Dr. Loraine Boettner quotes Dr. J. G. Vos's definition: "Amillennialism is that view of the last things which holds the Bible does not predict a "millennium" or period of world-wide peace and righteousness on this earth before the end of the world. (Amillennialism teaches that there will be a parallel and contemporaneous development of good and evil— God's kingdom and Satan's kingdom—in this world, which will continue until the second coming of Christ. At the second coming of Christ, the resurrection and judgment will take place, followed by the eternal order of things—the absolute, perfect kingdom of God, in which there will be no sin, suffering or death)" (p. 4).

B. POSTMILLENNIALISM

The prefix "post" means "after" the millennium and describes the idea that Jesus will return to earth after society has been Christianized by the church.

The Lord will come to earth after man establishes the kingdom. The thousand-year reign of Christ is not taken literally.

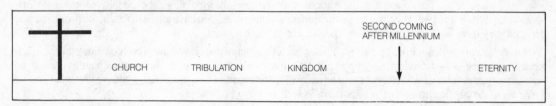

SECOND COMING
AFTER MILLENNIUM

CHURCH　　　　TRIBULATION　　　　KINGDOM　　　　　　　　　　　　　ETERNITY

Besides the amil and postmil views, there exists the premillennial or premil viewpoint. It is upon this perspective that most of the recent popular books on prophecy have been written.

C. PREMILLENNIALISM

The prefix "pre" means "before" the millennium. It describes the concept that after the tribulation Jesus will return to earth and establish His kingdom on the earth for a thousand years.

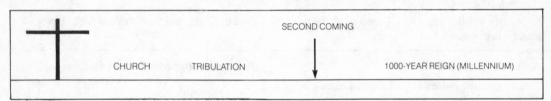

SECOND COMING

CHURCH　　　　TRIBULATION　　　　　　　　　　1000-YEAR REIGN (MILLENNIUM)

Dr. J. Dwight Pentecost defines this position as "…the view that holds that Christ will return to earth, literally and bodily, before the millennial age begins and that, by His presence, a kingdom will be instituted over which He will reign. In this kingdom all of Israel's covenants will be literally fulfilled. It will continue for a thousand years, after which the kingdom will be given by the Son to the Father when it will merge with His eternal kingdom. The central issue in this position is whether the Scriptures are to be fulfilled literally or symbolically" (*Things to Come*, p. 372).

In the beginning of this book I mentioned that just as all of the other prophecies about Jesus had been fulfilled literally and in great detail, so will those prophecies yet to be fulfilled. Therefore I hold to the premillennial view—that Jesus will return to earth after the tribulation to set up a literal kingdom on earth.

However, the major concern of most people interested in prophecy is not so much when the *millenium* will occur as it is when the *rapture* will take place.

The rapture is the great escape from Planet Earth, when Jesus returns to the air and removes the church from this planet *(1 Thessalonians 4:17)*. The concern of many Christians is when Jesus will return for His own. And as believers differ on the millennial issue, so they differ on the rapture question.

What are the major viewpoints regarding the rapture and tribulation? The four most popular views are the pretribulation, posttribulation, midtribulation, and partial-rapture beliefs.

1. Partial-rapture view

Those who hold to this view are in one sense pretribulationists, because they expect the rapture to occur before the tribulation. However, they expect that believers will be raptured in groups during the tribulation as they are prepared to go. They base their view on such passages as *Philippians 3:20, Titus 2:13,* and *2 Timothy 4:8.*

Dr. Walvoord argues against this view on three bases: a) it is based on a works principle, in opposition to Scriptural teaching on grace; b) it divides the body of Christ; and c) it ignores the plain teaching concerning the translation of all true believers when the event takes place (*The Rapture Question*, pp. 24-25).

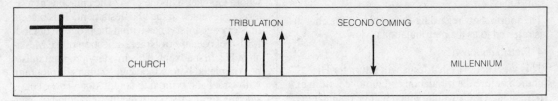

A second common view as to when the rapture will occur is the posttribulation perspective.

2. Posttribulation view

Recently this view has become quite popular. The word "post" means "after" the tribulation, expressing the idea that Jesus will come for His church after the tribulation. In other words, the church will go through the tribulation.

Robert H. Gundry, Professor of New Testament and Greek at Westmont College in Santa Barbara, California, is an exponent of this view. He writes, "The issue which we are approaching has to do with the possibility of Jesus' return to evacuate the church from the earth before a future period of intense tribulation. If we favor the possibility of such a pre-tribulational rapture, it becomes incumbent to stand in constant readiness for the event. However, if Jesus will return solely after the tribulation, that readiness should include mental and moral preparation for prior experience of the tribulation itself. The exhortation to 'endure to the end' and the special warning about the leading astray of, 'if possible, even the elect' *(Matthew 24:12,13,24)* highlight the danger of dismay and loss of faith on the part of whatever saints do find themselves in the last great time of testing" *(The Church and the Tribulation*, p. 9).

A posttribulational time line would look something like the following:

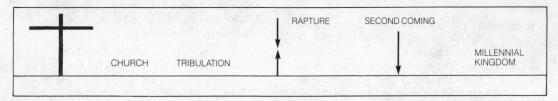

3. Midtribulation view

A third view, less prominent than posttribulationism, is the midtribulation view. The idea conveyed by this view sees the church passing through the first half of the tribulation. Then Jesus will rapture it in the middle of the tribulation.

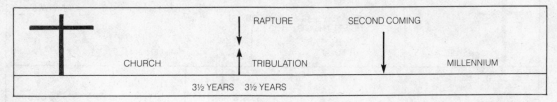

This viewpoint was championed by Dr. Norman B. Harrison many years ago, but has found few adherents today.

The fourth view regarding the rapture of the church is referred to as the pretribulational view.

4. Pretribulation view

This view believes that Jesus will return for His church before the tribulation and remove it from experiencing God's wrath, which will be poured out on the earth.

Dr. J. Dwight Pentecost writes about the essential basis of this view. "Pretribulation rapturism rests essentially on one major premise—the literal method of interpretation of the Scriptures....The church and Israel are two distinct groups with whom God has a divine plan. The church is a mystery, unrevealed in the Old Testament. This present mystery age intervenes within the program of God for Israel because of Israel's rejection of the Messiah at His first advent. This mystery program must be completed before God can resume His program with Israel and bring it to completion. These considerations all arise from the literal method of interpretation" (*Things to Come*, p. 193).

The pretribulational time chart places the rapture before the tribulation.

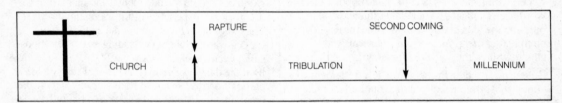

I personally hold to this view, because I believe that it most consistently answers many of the difficulties associated with the interpretation of prophetic passages.

I suggest three primary reasons why the pretribulational view has satisfied my own curious mind. The first reason is that it allows a literal interpretation of all Old and New Testament passages regarding the great tribulation. The church is not going to experience God's program for Israel or for the world.

A second reason for the pretribulational view is that the tribulation is the period in which God prepares Israel for its restoration *(Jeremiah 30:4-11)*, and at a time when God's wrath is poured out on sinful man *(Revelation 16:11)*. In contrast, the Bible promises that the church is not appointed to experience God's wrath *(Romans 5:9, 1 Thessalonians 1:9,10; 5:9)* and will in fact be delivered from the hour of trial *(Revelation 3:10)*.

Another reason for the pretribulational view is that the judgment seat of Christ best fits into God's chronology between the rapture and the second coming of Christ. While sinful man experiences God's wrath on earth, believers will be at the *bema* seat in heaven to be rewarded for their faithfulness. A complete time chart showing all of the major events is as follows.

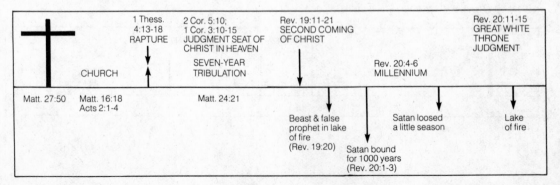

As I conclude this book, I want to point out several dangers that we need to avoid when we consider the final events of history.

First, we should avoid making our views concerning the chronology of the rapture or understanding of the second coming a basis for fellowship. Many people hold views because of how they were taught rather than as a result of personal investigation. Also, many committed believers have studied the Scriptures thoroughly and interpret the evidence differently. That is no reflection on a person's spirituality. It merely reflects his understanding of the facts.

Secondly, just because many good Christians hold differing viewpoints, we should not conclude that it doesn't matter what we believe about future things. That's a cop-out. It is important that we study the Scriptures and select a view which best answers our own questions and is faithful to the rules of interpretation.

A third danger which we need to avoid concerns itself with what we do with our knowledge of prophetic truth. Once our curiosity about future events has been satisfied, what will we do with that truth?

Prophetic knowledge should cause us to change our character or our behavior.

1. Look up the following references and write out what your response should be in light of prophetic truth.

a) *Matthew 24:42-44* _____

_____

_____

_____

b) *Philippians 4:5* _____

_____

_____

c) *Philippians 1:9,10* _____

_____

_____

_____

d) *Philippians 3:20,21* _____

_____

_____

_____

e) *1 Corinthians 4:5* _____

_____

_____

_____

f) *Acts 3:19-21* _____

_____

_____

_____

g) *Matthew 16:24-27* _____

_____

_____

_____

h) *1 Thessalonians 5:2-6* _____

_____

_____

_____

i) *2 Timothy 4:1,2* _____

_____

_____

_____

j) *1 John 3:2,3* _____

_____

_____

_____

k) *1 John 2:28* _____

_____

_____

_____

l) *1 Peter 1:7* _____

_____

_____

2. Of the three major views on the millennium, which view do you most favor? Why? _____

_____

_____

_____

3. Of the four major views concerning the rapture and tribulation, which view do you most favor? Why? _____

_____

_____

_____

4. In what way have you been helped most by this study? _____

_____

_____

_____

5. List the names of five individuals who could profit from a study on prophecy (Christian or non-Christian).

a) _____

b) _____

c) _____

d) _____

e) _____

6. List several ways in which you could encourage them to read and study prophecy.

a) _____

_____

_____

_____

b) _____

_____

_____

_____

c) _____

_____

_____

_____

When I was a young boy, my dad traveled from Lancaster to Pittsburgh, Pennsylvania, as a project engineer for a cork company. During much of that time I would see him only on weekends. Sunday evening was always a drag, because that's when he would leave for Pittsburgh. But Friday evenings were joyous occasions, because he would return to Lancaster and usually bring some gifts with him for my sisters and myself.

I remember many Friday evenings, waiting on the front porch in the summer or looking out the front window during the winter, anticipating Dad's arrival.

However, there were also those times when I had been a real terror around the house, teasing my sisters and getting into various kinds of mischief. On those occasions Mother would say, "You wait until your father comes home tonight. I plan to let him know just how you've been behaving!" Believe me, that sure changed my outlook on Dad's returns! No longer was I excited. In fact, I didn't want him to come home at all. I wasn't ready. My house wasn't in very good order.

Many people are in that same situation today. They are either ignorant that Jesus is coming again or else they know it but don't want to talk about it because it scares them.

Jesus' return can be an exciting event for you, with great reward, or it can be a terrifying experience. Your relationship to Him will determine which it will be.